STARS AND TEARS

Michel Pochet

STARS AND TEARS

A Conversation with Chiara Lubich

New City London

First published as
Dialogue avec Chiara Lubich 1983
by Nouvelle Cité, Paris

First published in Great Britain 1985
by Mariapolis Ltd.
57 Twyford Avenue, London W3 9PZ

ISBN 0 904287 25 4

Set in New York, U.S.A. by
New City Press
Printed and bound in Great Britain by
Biddles Ltd., Guilford, Surrey

Contents

FOREWORD

Although a biography of Chiara Lubich already exists, and despite the fact that nearly all of her spiritual writings have been translated into English, many people feel the need to know more about the spirituality, the Movement and the person of Chiara Lubich. This book, by Michel Pochet, grew out of precisely this need.

It presents a series of 'conversations', the material for which comes from speeches given on various occasions, private talks and interviews on television and radio, in newspapers and magazines.

The book was originally published in French in 1983 to mark the twenty-fifth anniversary of the Focolare Movement's presence in France and Belgium. In 1985 it is twenty-one years since the Movement arrived in Britain so this year, too, is a good occasion to publish these 'dialogues'—only, of course, in English!

INTRODUCTION

The name of Chiara Lubich occurs with increasing regularity among those of the main spiritual leaders of our time. However, it must be said that outside of her writings little is known about her. She is rarely seen, does not make public statements and does not habitually submit to being interviewed. Many have perceived however that on the religious scene she is a personality of the very first rank. They would like to understand her role better and get to know her more fully.

Chiara Lubich is at the head of a vast and complex movement still establishing itself and which numbers more than a million members in more than 150 nations. She has neither time nor strength to do other than occupy herself with it. However, she does not disdain either the press or the television. She does not fear debate, quite the contrary. But she places extreme confidence in those who on numerous occasions are led to speak in some way in her name.

In return it is quite natural that those who have this difficult task should be seen to be particularly attentive to what Chiara Lubich does and to what she is saying. They must maintain their union with her at its highest level. That astonishing confidence and the attitude which flows from it are quite obviously in complete contrast to the idolatry which some people seem to observe. On the contrary it is one of the most typical manifestations of the Focolare spirituality of community: freedom in unity.

It is in that spirit and thanks to that confidence that I publish this conversation with Chiara Lubich. In this year 1983 in fact, the publishing house *Nouvelle Cité* wanted to mark the fortieth anniversary of the founding of the Focolare Movement and the twenty-fifth year of its presence in France and Belgium with a book, which they asked me to put together. That is how this dialogue came to be.

I had at my disposal a bulky dossier of interviews, replies to readers of *Città Nuova*, addresses given on different occasions, a variety of texts often covering the same material, unsuitable for publishing as they stood and yet it would have seemed wicked to keep them to myself. Moreover I have known Chiara Lubich for nearly twenty-five years and every day these twenty-five years people have been asking me about the Focolare and the spirituality of the Movement. I live that spirituality myself, and as I ponder it, I know that it has transformed my way of seeing, speaking and acting.

This book then came into being as a dialogue going on in me, between people asking me questions and Chiara Lubich. It goes without saying that I have attributed no utterance to Chiara Lubich which was not perfectly authentic and which a little patience will permit the reader to discover in the printed documents.

I have endeavoured not to obtrude myself, so that the exchange should be as direct as possible, but of course it is I who asked the questions and I who searched here and there for elements of what seemed the appropriate response. And yet I know that so long a communion of heart and spirit authorises me to do so.

Michel Pochet
Easter 1983

PROLOGUE

You are the founder of the Focolare Movement. How did the idea come to you of starting that new form of christian life in community?

I must honestly admit that I never had any idea of founding a movement. The very idea seemed about as far away as the moon.

Yet the Movement exists and it is you, a lay person, a woman who founded it. How did it happen?

You remind me of an anecdote which illustrates very well my feelings about the founding of the Movement.

Tell me the story.

In 1968 I was in a remote area of Cameroon in the middle of the jungle, where the tribe of the Bangwa lived; they were heading for extinction then because of infant mortality. Three of my friends had gone before me to provide some help for those suffering the greatest deprivation. I had the chance to speak to Fon, the chief of the tribe, who although he knew little of the world, had been informed of the existence of the Movement. Impressed by its enormously wide diffusion over five continents he enquired of me in these terms: "You are a woman and so you are worth nothing. Tell me then how all this happened?" "You are a woman and so you are worth nothing." That way of putting it did not upset me in the least, because I knew that what I had to tell him was certainly not the work of a woman but the work of God.

All the same, you came into this story in the first person. It is a work that God has done no doubt, but he used you to do it.

The pen does not know what it will write, the artist's brush does not know what it will paint nor the chisel how the sculptor will use it. And similarly, when God takes someone in hand to bring a new work into being, that person does not know what he will achieve; he is simply an instrument. And that, I think, is my story. The Movement has all the characteristics of a work of God; unconditional unity with the leaders of the Church, fruitfulness and a rate of growth beyond what could be expected of human capacity or genius, experiences of the cross also, but above all a great abundance of fruit.

The instruments which God chooses display in general one common feature: smallness, weakness. Paul says that "God has chosen the weak things of the world... so that no man might boast before God." While that person works away in God's hands, God is forming him, shaping him in thousands and thousands of ways, both joyful and painful. Until the day when, having acquired a profound knowledge of himself and a certain intuition of God, that person can say with conviction: I am nothing; God is everything.

I
THE STORY OF AN IDEAL

It was wartime and everything was falling apart. In the face of that tragic situation, some of your friends and yourself decided to give your lives for something which does not pass away; for God. That is how you usually tell the story of the origins of the Focolare Movement. But how did the adventure start? What sparked it off?

It all began one morning in December 1943. Mother asked me to run a small errand for her. (I was to go to the dairy in a hamlet called *Madonna Bianca* about a mile or so from our house.) To please her I set out, and on the way I felt a call; it was as if God were saying to me, "Give yourself to me." I stood still in the middle of the road: I was so struck by this unexpected thought that had come to me. As soon as I got home again I wrote to my confessor who, a few days later, gave me permission to consecrate myself to God for life.

Did your confessor raise no objections? It is not usual to obtain permission to consecrate oneself for good and all straight away. Normally the Church is very careful and requires temporary vows before life vows are made.

I did not know that such complicated things existed in the church; I went to see him, convinced that everything would go smoothly. But at one point the priest began to ask me a series of questions: had I thought it over properly, had I thought of this or that? I replied that I had, and he continued: "Do you realise that your brother and your sisters will get married, they will have children, your parents will die and you will end up all alone in the old folks' home and you'll have nobody?"

What a cheerful prospect! That's what is called playing the devil's advocate! You would need to have an authentic vocation to resist such arguments.

He spoke to me so forcefully and in such an unexpected way that I couldn't make sense of anything any more, I wondered whether the priest was opposed to my intention. Then I said: "But I'm asking for nothing but to do what God wants." And he said: "No, you must tell me what *you* want!" Then I thought to myself that as long as there was a tabernacle on earth I would never be alone and I replied: "If it only depends on me, I will consecrate myself to God." I remember that was an extraordinary, an exceptional day. I had married God. I expected everything from Him but I had no idea of what the future held. There was such a joy in me that day, such a fire, suddenly lit, secret, that I did not want to tell anyone what had happened. In spite of everything the joy was visible, contagious. The proof was that my companions felt that flame when they met me and they wanted to follow me into that attraction which God was exerting on me.

That far-off day, the 7th of December 1943, at once so simple and so extraordinary, can you not describe it? Of course, for you it was a moment of intimacy with God, difficult to share, but it was also the birth of the Movement and therefore highly significant.

Imagine a girl in love, feeling that love which is the first, the purest, love as yet undeclared but which has begun to burn; with one single difference. When a young girl is thus in love on this earth, she has before her the face of her beloved, whereas one in love with God does not see him, does not touch him; she does not breathe the perfume of his presence with the senses of the body but with those of the soul, through which love has entered and has invaded her completely. Hence this special joy of which I was speaking and which it is rare to experience a second time in one's life, a secret, serene, exultant joy.

A few days before 7th December I had been told to keep a vigil before the crucifix on the preceding night in order to prepare me better for my wedding with God, a wedding which was to be celebrated in the most secret way. Only God, my confessor and myself knew what was happening.

That evening I tried to keep a vigil, kneeling at the bedside before a metal crucifix. I prayed, I think, about two hours. But I was young and not very convinced of the value of certain practices which later on turned out not to be in conformity with my vocation. I fell asleep —but not without noticing that the crucifix had grown all misty from my breath as I prayed.

I saw a sign in this; the Crucified One whom I was to follow would not be so much the Christ with the physical wounds which many spiritualities emphasise, but rather the Christ of spiritual sufferings.

In the morning I got up towards five o'clock. I put on my best dress and set off, right across the town, towards a little convent. I had previously warned my mother that I had to go to a ceremony that would be rather long.

A storm was raging, so severe that I had to struggle along holding my umbrella in front of me. These circumstances were not without meaning. They expressed—it seemed to me—that the deed which I was carrying out would encounter obstacles. That tempest of wind and rain against me struck me as the sign of a hostile power.

On my arrival at the convent the scene changed. An enormous portal opened on its own, automatically. I had an impression of relief and welcome, like the wide open arms of this God who was awaiting me. The little chapel was decorated and looked its best. At the back a statue of the Virgin stood out. Before the altar, in the choir, someone had thoughtfully placed a *prie-dieu*.

The priest had told me to prepare a little folded note in which I was to ask for a favour, which I might be sure of obtaining on a day like that. He took it (on the note I had asked for the gift of faith for someone who was dear to me) he put it under the chalice and the Mass began.

Before communion, I saw in a moment what I was doing: in consecrating myself to God I had crossed a bridge; the bridge was crumbling away behind me; never again would I be able to return to the world. Yes, because my consecration was not simply a formula like the one which I had read before the Host elevated before me: "I make the vow of perfect and perpetual chastity." It was something else: I was being married to God. That meant not only celibacy, renouncing human marriage. It meant leaving all, parents, studies, school, entertainment, everything in my little universe that I had loved up to then. This sudden insight into what I was doing was brief, but so powerful that a big tear fell onto the open page of my missal.

Mass finished in silence. I came down from the choir and knelt at a pew. The priest took off his vestments and knelt a few pews behind me. A long prayer of thanksgiving. Then coming over to me the priest said, "You will be a bride of blood." Although I was grateful for anything that might be said to me, these words were at variance with what I was feeling deeply within me. That expression "Bride of blood" struck me as anachronistic, it did not seem to be made for me. And my heart replied, "No, I am the bride of God." And it was this God who was to reveal himself later as the Forsaken One. Blood indeed, but blood of the soul.

I think I ran the whole way home. I only stopped near the bishop's home to buy three red carnations for the crucifix which was waiting for me in my room. They were the sign of the common festival. That was all.

That was just the beginning, but by the following year you already had companions wanting to follow you.

Some months passed and then on May 13th 1944 a terrible bombardment ravaged the city of Trent. In the evening during the alert my family decided to leave the city and go and camp in a wood on a hill called *Goccia d'oro*. During the night, we saw the aircraft flying over Trent and bombing our district. That was a decisive night for me. It seemed to me that the Lord was asking me to leave everything, even my parents. "He who does not leave father, mother, wife, children and lands cannot be my disciple." In fact I understood within myself that I could not leave Trent even if my home were destroyed. The link which had formed between my friends and myself was so strong that I could do nothing other than stay put.

Taking such a decision was, however, a real dilemma quite simply because I dearly loved my parents, and my brothers and sisters, and being the only breadwinner I could not see how to leave them. A saying which I had learned at school came into my head *"Omnia vincit amor"* "Love conquers all."

"How?" I asked myself. Can love conquer this too? Am I to abandon my own people who are going to leave for the mountains? And in my heart, with his help, I immediately said yes to Jesus. The following day at dawn we returned to our house to survey the damage. There was nothing left but the walls. We had to clamber over the debris to recover a few objects and put them in rucksacks. I had to speak to my parents, to tell them of my decision. I went to find Father in the kitchen, knelt down and said, "Father, I belong to God, and others are following me; I cannot leave." My father must have been granted a special grace for he gave me his blessing with perfect calm and allowed me to stay.

The most harrowing moment was the parting, when I had to abandon my loved ones and place on my mother's tired shoulders the rucksack which I was to have carried.

I went back towards the town. The destruction was total, trees uprooted, houses in ruins, roads covered with debris. Tears came to my eyes . . . and I let them flow.

Suddenly a woman appeared at the corner of a street, grabbed hold of me and began to shout in a frenzy: "They're dead, all four of them! Do you understand, all four of them!"

I comforted her and realised that I must silence my own grief in order to take on that of others.

It was six o'clock in the morning and the streets were deserted. I began to look for my friends. They were all alive, thank God. At that time we formed a little group of six or seven girls aged between fifteen and twenty-three.

And what became of your parents?

Long afterwards they told me that they had scarcely turned their backs on Trent to go away when they suddenly felt a great joy. They began to joke and laugh. They walked for a few miles and soon found shelter with two ladies.

Your home was in ruins, you were alone on the street exposed to devastation and in mourning. The situation was dramatic, and yet to hear you speaking about the war one gets the impression that you have some good memories of those days spent in the shelters.

They were unforgettable days, among the best in my life. The air-raid shelter where we took refuge was not very safe. It was an excavation under a rock, solid enough fortunately, but without a door. If a bomb had fallen in front of it we should all have been dead. The air-raid warnings came one after another night and day, up to eleven in a single day. People only went back to their houses long enough to fetch necessities and then scurried away again with all speed. My companions already made up a fine group; they had the courage to go right across the city when the sirens wailed in order to assemble in the shelter where I was, and if need be to die together.

As there was no question of doing otherwise, I took the gospels which we read in a corner of the shelter with the people who were taking refuge there. And the Gospel was opened up to us, in the sense that all its words were illuminated. I saw them light up one after another as if they were completely new and I had never read them before. At the same time as the Lord was giving me this light, he was encouraging me to live. He enlightened my spirit and encouraged my will. I attribute this fact to the presence of Jesus who, as at Emmaus, explained the Scriptures to his disciples. One after another we took up these words which had touched us as if we were hearing them for the first time, even though in fact we had already heard them often on the lips of excellent preachers. We were able, without delay, to put them into practice, because our neighbour was always there. Those who were suffering were right beside us, the mother with her children was there, a few feet away. Then one of my companions would take a child in her arms and look after it, another would help the old people or get them something to eat. We would hurry home to make soup in an enormous pot and then we would run to distribute it among the poor. The poor were our brothers. They came to us. And all around you would see little groups of two, a focolarina and someone in need.

Once, the shelter was badly shaken. Bombs fell just above and to the side of the opening. The shelter was filled with thick dust. We were lying face down stretched out on the ground. A single idea came to me, the meaning of which I did not understand; I would be sorry to die without having had the time to finish a 'Hail Mary'.

Later when the Movement grew, its members like beads in a living rosary, I understood what the pain I experienced that day had meant; it was the pain of not being able to contribute to building a work for Mary which would be hers.

What kind of life did the first community lead, the first focolare?

Beautiful, beautiful. You only had to go in . . . It was very poor accommodation because we had reduced it to a strict minimum. We had got rid of the few pieces of furniture which we possessed by giving them to the poor. In our bedroom we had kept only our sprung mattresses which we laid on top of tins of the powdered milk which was issued to us during the war, and, pinned on the wall, a picture of Jesus Forsaken. As soon as we woke our eyes turned at once to that picture and we would murmur, "Because you are forsaken" as if to say, "I live because you are forsaken, my reason for living is your forsakenness."

How was your life organised?

Like that of a family. At the beginning I was still a student. I remember my last day's study. It was for a geography course and I had laid out atlases and notebooks on the floor.

I was sitting on a sheepskin rug that we had been given. I did not know that I was studying for the last time but I wanted to make a masterpiece of this piece of work. I studied each paragraph minutely, not so much because the material interested me but because God interested me, and as at that moment I had to study, loving God meant studying. Apart from my study at University I was responsible for preparing meals for the focolarine. One of them worked in a butcher's shop, one in an office, others elsewhere, but all of them returned at midday for lunch.

That day I was making some particularly appetising soup because I had been a little generous with the seasoning, and while the soup was simmering I was revising my geography. Thirteen times already I had been told to stop my studies because the Movement had come into being and was already demanding my full attention. However, each time I had been asked to resume my studies. But the fourteenth time did the trick and I was pleased after the event to have studied so conscientiously for what was to be the last time. That day I finally put my books up in the attic packed away in a box.

Was everything always rosy then?

Unity was not always perfect of course. Unity has to be earned; it demands death to oneself, not only mortification, but being "dead" so that Jesus may live in us.

One morning we had parted a little brusquely to go to work and I had stayed at home feeling that Jesus was no longer present in our midst. It was as if everything was crumbling away. I couldn't understand any more why I had left my parents whom I loved so much, nor why I had given up my studies. Nothing made sense to me any more. I went up to the attic to fetch wood for the stove in order to prepare a meal for the focolarine. I saw my dear books again and I wept over those old volumes. The tears as they fell disturbed the dust. At that moment I remembered my reason for living: unity, Jesus. If I was feeling all these things it was because our bond as brethren had disappeared with the departure of our Brother. So as soon as my companions came back, the first thing to be done was to recall our Brother to our midst. In that way everything would become clear again.

I went back downstairs, put the finishing touches to the meal, and when the others arrived I said to them, "One of us is guilty of a fault; if it's me I ask you to forgive me." We all begged each other's forgiveness and Jesus returned among us. I saw afresh that that was worth having left everything, studies, parents, a future family, everything, and that was the end of the matter.

Did your community have a rule? Did you have days of recollection?

What a funny idea! We met on all our free days, for example we spent Sundays together. We would recount our experiences. We would go deeply into some point of the spirituality of the gospel. And if we found anything beautiful we would share it.

But above all we were a family. For example I would plait the hair of one of my companions if she had difficulty doing her own hair. We would iron skirts or blouses for each other. As my stomach was a little delicate Natalia used to bake very light bread specially for me.

The rule was love, life. The rule was Jesus in the midst. It was so real that much later, towards 1955 or 1956 I had the feeling of being present at a miracle. It was at Tonadico. About sixty boys and girls who wanted to consecrate themselves to God had gathered in the church. On entering I got the impression that they formed a body which *knew* how to live, without, for all that, having an external, written law. They had no rule, and yet already they knew how to live.

What did the people of the town say?

Reactions varied. The poor welcomed us with open arms; many people followed us, from every walk of life. Of course I knew as time went on that certain of them criticized us because they thought that we were changing their religion. At the time we knew nothing of these criticisms, and indeed nothing would have changed if we had, so strong was the light of God. We would not have let ourselves be intimidated. And then we had a key to solve every problem: we loved our enemies.

You have spoken of your great love of study; surely your companions also had plans for the future.

We were young, and like all young people, each of us had an ideal. I remember one of my friends, who was anxiously waiting for the end of the war in order to get married. Unfortunately her fiancé never returned. Her whole ideal collapsed. Another had filled her house with tastefully chosen furniture but the bombs reduced her house to rubble. In spite of all my love for God I too had an ideal: study, and in particular, the study of philosophy.

As I told you, I had to put all my books in the attic. It was as if God were using the circumstances to teach us that all is vanity of vanities, that everything is passing.

Together we decided that God would be the ideal of our lives.

Again the question is, how you set about doing that. What, in practical terms did that choice mean for you?

The Gospel gave us the answer. "It is not he who says Lord, Lord, who will enter the kingdom of heaven but he who does the will of my Father who is in heaven."

Doing the will of the Father, the will of God and not our own, that is how to love God. We were carried by a forward momentum towards the fulfillment of the particular design that God had for each one of us, however little we accepted his plans.

But time was passing and young as we were, death was always before our eyes. It was then that an idea came to us: is there a particular desire on the part of God, so dear to the heart of Jesus that, should death come upon us suddenly, he would be pleased with us in our last moments? There too the Gospel gave us the answer. In the shelters we read these words: "I give you a new commandment: love one another as I have loved you. Greater love has no man than this, than to give up his life for his friends."

We said to ourselves, "So that is what is most particularly pleasing to God, this is that 'special will' that we were seeking. Let us live it and declare to each other 'I am ready to die for you, for her, she for you, any of us for the other, all for each one, so that we may love each other and live this new commandment.'"

It must be said that from that moment on, the occasions when we were literally risking our lives were not many! But what we could do every day was to share the suffering of one or the other.

There was no lack of suffering to share during the war.

I remember the day when we rediscovered the saying; "Whatever you have done to one of these little ones, who are my brothers, you have done to me." It was like a war cry, because we realised that in the poor, Christ was present. We began to go through the town as soon as we could—that is, in the intervals between bombardments—to look for the poor, to find where they lived, in order to help them, to comfort Jesus present in them. And lots of adventures came our way (gifts of clothes, blankets, flour, powdered milk, firewood. . . .)

Another word from the gospel, one of the first which had touched us, had been "Give and it will be given to you." You should have seen our little house at that time. One day someone brought us apples. Immediately the poor got the benefit of them. On our return, there again were some apples. This sequence of events was repeated three times in succession, until, in the evening, a whole case full of apples arrived!

That was our day-to-day life, our daily lot. It was the same when we decided to live the word: "Ask and it will be given to you." At that time we had already realised that Jesus is present in a particular way in every person. One day a poor man confided to me that he needed a pair of shoes. He took a size 42. Then with that completely new faith which God had given us I went into a church and I said to Jesus: "Jesus, you need a pair of shoes, size 42, I am praying for them now." I left the church and bumped into a lady, who handed me a parcel.

And of course it was a pair of shoes of the right size!

Those concrete experiences, those confirmations of the gospel, its truth and its efficacy gave us wings. And there was another word: "May they all be one that the world might believe." It was enough that we should be one, that is, that we should love each other as he wished, for others to believe in God. How many began to believe simply through seeing the way of life of these young girls. How many vocations there were! How many inextricable situations were unravelled. At the end of two months there were five hundred of us from all areas, of all ages and every walk of life, adults and children. In the little town of Trent we could no longer go unnoticed. It was then that we went to our bishop, for we had found in the Gospel the words, "He who hears you hears me." The bishop was Christ's representative. If he told us to go ahead, well and good, but if he told us to stop everything we should have obeyed him with the same simplicity.

What was the bishop like?

He was a jovial person. He described himself as a "peddler of the grace of God" because everywhere in the Trent valleys he preached that people must be in a state of grace before God. He could seem harsh but, at the moment of taking leave of us, on the doorstep he said to us with a smile: "Make saints of yourselves, all of you—I mean it!" He was a man of God. He used to say to anyone who would listen: "When I appear before St. Peter, he will say to me: 'Come right in, you deserve it because you encouraged the focolarine.'" He has always looked after us and when the first two boys went to him to plan a men's focolare he replied at first: "Come back when there are three of you." Then, probably reading disappointment on Marco's face, he had second thoughts. "Oh, all right then, I'll be the third." When we went to see him for the first time and told him what was happening he interrupted me: "I understand. The teacher must remain the teacher, the mother must remain the mother, the office worker must remain the office worker,—and he added curiously—the executioner must remain an executioner and the bishop must remain a bishop, but all have to love each other, isn't that it?" "Yes that's it." "*Digitus Dei est hic*—The finger of God is here." And indeed that's how it was. There were still no structures but there was mutual love within the christian community.

At that period the focolare already existed, but previously, even before you had any companions, how did the first intuition of it come to you?

Well I must tell you about the intuition I had in 1939. I was at Loreto for a Catholic Action rally. The first time I went into the Holy House of Loreto I had no time to consider whether this was really the place where historically the Holy Family had lived. I knelt on the floor near the wall blackened by the smoke of the lamps. I couldn't utter a single word; I was seized by the mystery of what had happened in that place. All kinds of ideas about the Holy Family came to me. I said to myself; the child Jesus walked from there to there. The voice of Jesus echoed between these walls, and Mary must have sung here to rock her little child to sleep. Maybe it was Joseph who fixed the beams in place. There was also a window; it came to me that maybe Mary was there at the moment of the Annunication and that the Angel came in at that window. All these thoughts pressed down on me, heavier and heavier. It was as if someone had placed the dome of St. Peter's on top of me, and I wept until I could weep no more.

That was the intuition that came to you in 1939. But now, after all these years, how do you see the family of Nazareth?

I can picture them to myself because I live in the focolare, which reproduces in some way the presence of Jesus among men. When Jesus is there we feel an extraordinary peace, a light illuminates us from within, we feel on top form, ready to venture anything, afraid of nothing. Thus if you can think that at Nazareth Jesus was physically present with Mary who was who she was, and with Joseph, who was also someone special, you can imagine what an extraordinary family the Trinity had thought up for the incarnation of the Word!

Was that episode at Loreto the beginning of the revelation of your particular vocation?

No, no! Definitely not. I was completely passive in the face of what was happening to me. It was simply that the Holy House at Loreto so attracted me that every time I could escape from my companions I rushed there and the same phenomenon was repeated. I think I stayed at Loreto a week or maybe longer. On the last day, when I was at the back of the basilica which is built over the house, the nave was full of young girls celebrating the conclusion of the rally, (wearing white veils, I remember) and an idea crossed my mind: an army of virgins will follow you.

And then I returned home. I met my confessor, who, seeing me quite content and at peace asked,

"Have you found your way?"

"Yes."

"Are you getting married?"

"No."

"Are you going to lead a consecrated life in the world?"

"No."

"Then are you entering a convent?"

"No, there is a fourth way."

Of course I knew nothing about this 'fourth way,' and that is the only moment when I had the intuition that others would follow me.

Does the religious family which has formed since correspond to the intuition of 1939?

It is not a religious family but a simple current of christian life, because all Christians must—or ought to—love one another. However at the heart of this vast Movement there is a nucleus which is not a convent but, shall we say, a form of community life, the focolare. The members of the focolare make vows, but they remain none the less lay people. There are also married people who commit themselves according to their state of life by promises of chastity, poverty, and obedience.

The first married person to have done so was Igino Giordani, whom you consider one of the founders of the Movement. He died in 1980 at the age of 86. He is little known outside Italy except to specialists. The biblical scholar Lagrange mentioned him as a "master among the Italian catholic writers." The academician Daniel-Rops compared him to Léon Bloy and Péguy. As a writer of note, a valued political figure and a Christian eager for holiness and unity, Giordani is undoubtedly one of the great Christian personalities of our time. I should be glad if you would talk about this outstanding individual.

To be the founder or even co-founder of a work which the Church recognizes as her own, involves an infinitely manifold and complex action of the grace of God, promptings of the Holy Spirit which are particularly varied and effective. It implies also in the person concerned conduct which is decisive for that work, attitudes most often unforeseen because they are suggested from above. It calls also for suffering, often piercing and prolonged and of course rare gifts of insight and love. So it is preferable to entrust to the history of the Church and to that of the spiritual movements which embellish it from century to century, the task of revealing such a personality. Despite that, it is possible—without in any way denying the difficulty of doing so—to talk a little about Igino Giordani as a focolarino.

Giordani was a man with a highly cultured religious faith. In the simple life of the Movement, in the Christian community of Trent which he had known towards the end of the 'forties, he had discovered the same principles as those stated by the Fathers of the Church in former centuries. He talked of being particularly touched by that and said that he naturally wanted to be a member of that community. But a new vocation was to owe its inception to him. How did that happen?

He came to lunch once at the focolare in Rome. I was facing him, and there were focolarine sitting round the table. He was speaking of virginity as a sublime thing. Perhaps because "He who humbles himself shall be exalted," I felt myself impelled to say to him: "At heart, what God is asking of us is love. All right, we have made the vow of chastity but that, after all, is only to help us love better, that there may be fewer obstacles to love; what stops you from being a focolarino if love is what counts?" That is how he became the first married focolarino. We brought him into the focolare, taking account of course of the obligations of his circumstances. Others followed him, and so well have they fitted into the focolare that I have come to realise that they were essential if the focolare was not to be confined to celibates only and was to retain as its model the Holy House of Loreto. In the focolare can be found an expression of fatherhood and motherhood in the spirit of virginity in the image of Joseph, the real husband of Mary and yet a virgin, and in that of Mary, virgin yet mother of Christ. That is the origin of the promises which the married focolarini make, after a time of probation, promises of poverty, chastity and obedience. . . in accordance with their married state.

So it was on that very day that the idea of the promises was born, for if I have understood it correctly, the married people already belonged to the focolare at least in a common search for the "perfection of charity." Giordani knew very well what that was all about.

As far as we can judge, he was perfect in love. And in such a delicate way that those who got close to him even thought he had a special gift for it. He really lived up to the nickname that he was given in the Movement, *Foco,* fire—that is the love at once supernatural and natural, for God and one's neighbour, which is at the base and at the summit of the Christian life. So he contributed in a unique way to keeping alive among us the Gospel verse which had been given to him when he joined the Movement, "Love one another as I have loved you." That is a word of life which it now seems that he left to us all like a final injunction, a testament. Even as death approached, Igino Giordani felt the love of God for him. "God," he used to say, "I see him as a Giver." Then he would give you a list of the gifts he had received from God. That love of God whom he contemplated led him in his turn to pour out his love on everyone else.

You like to talk of him as a man of the beatitudes.

He was "pure in heart" in an exceptional way. That is why he could open up for married people, men or women from all over the world, an original kind of consecration to God in a spiritual virginity achieved by the most ardent charity.

That purity of heart had refined and intensified his most noble emotions. Listening to him, seeing him in action, you could understand the words of St. Thérèse of Lisieux: "When the heart gives itself to God, it does not lose its tenderness. On the contrary, the tenderness grows, becomes purer and more divine."

Giordani had a very tender love for his wife. It was moving to see the strikingly intense affection that he had for his four children and for his grandchildren too. He was an exemplary father and grandfather, a man wholly given to God.

He was "poor in spirit" in a complete detachment not only from everything he possessed but above all from everything that he was.

And he was full of mercy. In his presence the most hardened sinner felt himself forgiven and the poorest felt like a king. One of the most striking features of his personality and one to which his political activity bears witness was to be a "peacemaker". He had acquired such meekness that you could understand from his example what the Gospel says: "Blessed are the meek for they shall inherit the earth." His gentleness, stamped with nobility, the way he would set about something, his own very special way of talking to each person, reached the hearts of everyone who came near him.

Everyone, no matter who, felt valued and at ease in his company, and even the young people succeeded in establishing a relationship with him of equal to equal.

In the course of his life he had known suffering both in soul and in body. But he had been able to transform the suffering into love and while he was yet on this earth God had already delivered him from all pain.

He "hungered and thirsted after justice". It was justice that he struggled for all his life, and it was because of the name of God that he was persecuted. That is why, today, we believe he is in possession of the Kingdom.

A Christian of the first order, a scholar, apologist, apostle, it seemed to him that he had found a fountain of pure water springing up from the Church to bear witness afresh to the vitality and ever-present activity of the Holy Spirit in her. Now he could "sell all his goods" to follow Jesus, who was calling him to quench his thirst at that water.

Day by day we saw his humility demonstrated. He had achieved the goal which he had set himself in 1941; "humility and charity". "To be at the service of all. To feel myself to be inferior to all, for the image of God is in everyone and Christ died for all. Only pride makes a man lonely and sad."

If it seemed to him that in the Movement some privilege was being accorded to him because of his past he would beg to be treated like all the others.

It makes you wonder how he could reach such heights, achieve that objective, while remaining youthful up to an advanced age and never seeming to grow old.

Simply because he who loves remains eternally young. Only he who does not love grows old, and as for the one who hates, he is already dead, as Giordani himself often declared. For those who knew him such a question holds no mysteries. His life, beyond all doubt, was a leap into God who is love. However he still did not neglect the means that the Church in her age long experience commends to those who would draw closer to God, the evangelical counsels. In our times certain practices are neglected, under-valued or considered cumbersome. A man of great intelligence and full of experience, Igino Giordani, out of his familiarity with numerous saints, whose lives he had written about, chose precisely those means to support his spiritual ascent and he loved them passionately.

St. Catherine of Siena whom he had greatly admired since his youth had taught him to "bind himself tightly" in obedience. Indeed says the saint, "with certain people, the gentle fire of love for holy obedience so grows, that hating themselves and desiring the complete destruction of their own will, they wish to bind themselves even more tightly." He had greatly suffered from what appeared to him as the spiritual marginalisation of the laity; as if sanctity were a preserve of convents or seminaries. Also he desired with all his heart—and he was great-hearted—to open the doors, to break down the partitions between those who lived in the state of perfection and others who—he would say humourously—were in a state of "imperfection". He was extremely sensitive to the signs of the times. More than that, he was himself, so to speak, a sign of the times, of these times in which the Holy Spirit—by the Second Vatican Council and many other means—is calling all the people of God to holiness. As one of the greatest Italian specialists in patristics, he often referred to the Fathers, and to St. John Chrysostom in particular, according to whom the married man must live just as the monk lives, apart from celibacy.

Nine days before his death Igino Giordani dictated a letter, which he addressed to a person who represented for him the authority of the Church. Among other things he wrote: "I am waiting to be able to do the will of God as you will declare it to me. I am waiting for a sign from you, for I want above all not to make a mistake. Of course, I do not want to push beyond the limits my need to obey. I beg you then urgently to give me your attention. I do not want the will of God to withdraw."

When Igino Giordani encountered the Movement, the women's and men's focolare were made up only of celibates. It was he who opened the door to people, who following him, felt a thirst for holiness and consecration. He took steps to bring to fruition the plan—hitherto no more than a distant prospect—of a community life, in so far as it was possible, comprising both celibates and married people, in the image of the family of Nazareth.

After the death of his wife in 1973 Giordani pressed to the limit the logic of his commitment and at the age of almost 80, began a community life in the strict sense in the focolare, "twenty-four hours a day" as he used to say. Can someone still change or develop at that age?

The focolare worked on him like a metal which had to be purified in two fires: the voice of Christ in his innermost self and the light of Christ present among his brethren.

His independent nature had led him to become an agressive apologist. In his youth he had left the secondary school for seminarists so as not to have to obey. But his nature surrendered finally and joyously while he travelled that last part of the road which brought him to God through his brethren, as the Movement teaches. And he declared himself free.

Back in 1954 he had written: "To be sacrificed, enclosed, dead to the world. While still being a layman, to be a religious in my soul, offered to God. To practise the evangelical counsels within the limits of possibility. If poverty, obedience, chastity arouse the anger of Satan and of men, if they bring with them humiliation and non-comprehension, to say joyfully like the psalmists: 'All is good for me that humbles me.' Not to squander the only life that is given us on making money, coveting power or other vanities, but to be burned up, consumed, like a lamp on the altar of Christ. Let every act, every word be love. Let even my breathing, my work, every human relationship be love. May the suffering which comes with being consumed produce love, even if with Christ, Love crucified, I must cry 'My God, my God, why have you forsaken me?'. "

I should like now on my own account to put to you the question of the king of the Bangwa. How can you, a woman, put yourself at the head of such a vast and complex Movement where there are men, women, young people, priests, religious, etc.?

I'll let St. Paul answer that for you. "There is no longer male nor female, Jew nor Greek, free man nor slave;" we are all equal. When I work for the Movement I don't think of myself as a woman, but before anything else as a disciple of Christ.

You have never married; your time has been taken up by the Movement. Could it be said that you have chosen something more important than being a wife and mother?

Yes. Although the calling of motherhood is a great one, I think that of the spiritual mother is even greater. I would just like to remind you, that while I never got married, that was not so that I could devote myself to the Movement. I was called by God to be married to God; I did not know the Movement would be born.

Like a nun?

The current way of thinking assumes that it is only sisters, people who go into convents, who have chosen God. That is completely ridiculous! Every Christian is called to choose God. Only then, and with God, he has to be clear what the Father's plan is for his life: to marry or not, to work in one sector or another, etc. It is absolutely necessary that we take the mystique out of that kind of Christianity in which God does not have the first place in our lives.

The conversion which Christ demands consists precisely in giving God the first place. What the focolarini do, we are all called to do, fathers of families, M.P.'s, workmen, dustmen, mothers, children, everyone, otherwise we are not all Christians.

Some people consider you a saint. What do you think of that?

If there is one thing I'm sure of it's that I'm no saint. That's obvious! Yet I want to grow in holiness, because "What God desires is our sanctification." That's what is written and it goes for me, for you and for everyone.

The fundamental act of your life as you yourself have said was to marry God forty years ago. At what level now is that intimacy with God, with Jesus Christ?

I would like to say in response to that, that Jesus is everything to me. And if he is not, may he become it.

II
THE RULE OF RULES

What is the aim of the Focolare Movement? What message is it setting out to convey to the world of today?

We must read between the lines of human history to spot the myriad marks of God's watchful care for his children. Among the many expressions of that love I will single out one which many others before me have remarked upon: at intervals God uses one of his children to proclaim anew one of his words in his Church and among humanity. That word is no banal utterance. It is his presence, God himself under the cover, if I can put it like that, of one of his words. And the word is what is called for at that moment in history. Remember for example how, when the wealth of certain churchmen sullied the face of the Bride of Christ, God cried, through Francis of Assisi the word "poverty".

At another time, a tragic moment in the Church's history, senior members of the hierarchy were enmeshed in a worldly and even immoral life. With the message of Catherine of Siena encapsulated in the words, "blood and fire," God reminded men that

Christ died for the salvation of every human being and that the Christian life must burn with love, set on fire by Christ. In an age of disruption and rebellion God raised up Ignatius of Loyola, who centred the life of his company upon obedience, and Theresa of Avila, whose writings and whose life say "prayer," because the times were so hard that only succour sought untiringly from God could help. And I could extend the list indefinitely.

Today the world is sick with a thousand divisions; separations between Christians, opposition between widely diverse ideologies, contrasting factions in the educational system, the breakdown of family life, the class struggle, to say nothing of the threat of worldwide catastrophe because of the failure of the two political blocs to get along with each other. I think God has raised up the Focolare Movement to shout at top volume, "Unity! That all may be one!"

Do you see any reason to hope that the message might be heard? Are you not afraid of crying in the wilderness?

Despite all these tensions our world is tending—and this is a paradox which we must recognise—towards unity. It's a sign of the times. The Holy Spirit is saying it and, after centuries of indifference and even hostility between them is pushing the Churches towards reunion. The Popes say it; Paul VI for example, whose teaching is imbued throughout with this idea of unity; and John-Paul II also—the pilgrim of unity—who beyond all doubt is moved by the Holy Spirit to undertake all these journeys and embrace the whole world in universal fashion, precisely to affirm that the Church is one, at the very moment when the differences which exist between the churches at a local level are becoming increasingly apparent.

The council also picked up this striving after unity in the world. Everywhere in its documents you come across the word 'unity.' Even ideologies which, as Christians, we cannot share, seek none the less to resolve the problems of the world on a global scale by the principle of unity; likewise the mass media, which bring the whole world into every home.

Really if we look at the world from God's angle we must draw the conclusion that it has a tendency towards unity.

So you conceived the Movement as a response to that aspiration to unity. Did you draw up a programme?

Not at all! I have never had a programme put together beforehand. The only architect of the Movement is God. I have followed him day by day. He suggested the first ideas to me about the spirituality and the structure of the Movement, his own ideas, which took shape when I spoke to my companions about them and which I submitted to the authorities before putting into practice. That's how the Movement spread in such a surprising way. At first silently in Italy, then from 1958, if I remember rightly, into other European nations and soon into the rest of the world. At present we have members in 156 different nations.

The Movement has surmounted not only political barriers, but also denominational barriers, some of them going back centuries. The Focolare Movement exists among Anglicans, Lutherans, Presbyterians, Orthodox and other christian denominations.

And the most beautiful thing about it is that the vocations which are springing up among the catholics are also to be found among the members of other Churches; there you will find focolarini, married focolarini, etc. and also movements like "New Families", "New Humanity", and the "Priests' Movement".

Naturally, in some parts of the world, the Movement has come into contact with the great non-christian religions. A dialogue of friendship and life has sprung up; members of the Movement have been able to get to know these brothers and sisters better, especially their sacred scriptures, and they have had a chance to discover the Gospel and our faith, with results that you can imagine.

But the men and women whom we have most at heart are the atheists of East and West; they are the poorest of all, because they lack God. The witness of our christian unity has touched many of them and they have turned to God.

What is it, in your opinion, that attracts followers to the Focolare Movement?

It's God. God, who is in the midst of the members of the Movement. Of course "in the midst" must not be understood in a physical sense; it is God present in each one of the members who are united. Yes it is God who draws us.

The religious life is in a state of crisis. How do you account for this attraction?

I can't put it into words for you. You would have to experience it for yourself. If you choose God as your Ideal you are at the same time deciding to follow him; I mean, to do what he brings your way.

That consists in substituting the will of God for your own will. And there's nothing magic about understanding what God wants in the present moment. It may be working, studying, going for a walk, playing, praying, listening to some good advice, or it could be following an idea which God puts into your heart, or again helping someone who needs you. . . .

What God puts above everything else is that you should love other people. Love is fundamental to the Gospel. Our attitude to others can only be one of love; even for our enemies. Read the Gospel and you will see.

And love brings with it the consequence that you understand many things. What you must do becomes clear to you. You grasp truths which you never paid any attention to before. You discover lots of things about God, because God takes what you do to others as done to him, and he rewards those who love him by giving them light. It is written: "To him who loves me I will manifest myself." It is this "manifestation" which makes God so attractive.

But what's new about that? After all, the commandment to love one another has been around a long time.

What was new forty years ago was perhaps the seriousness with which we loved each other. We were trying to live out the word which Jesus said just after giving his commandment: "There is no greater love than this, that a man should give his life for his friends."

We decided to be ready to die, the one for the other. That decision involved certain consequences. If we were ready to die we were obviously ready to share each other's sufferings, to bear each other's burdens, to have our spiritual and material goods in common like the first Christians. Not all Catholics did as much.

Even today we say to those whom we meet that they must be ready to die for one another, because the Gospel demands that, if you take it seriously.

You have set out the spiritual, internal reasons for the spread of the Movement. Could you describe the means through which that happens in practical terms?

The 'more excellent way', which must be fundamental to all the others, is love. Love for one's neighbour which springs, like cause and effect, from loving God.

The Movement has spread enormously because the personal relationships which formed between members of the Movement and their neighbour were guided by the Gospel: "Love your neighbour as yourself."

It is a matter of "making oneself one with the other" in a perfect renunciation of self, making the problems, suffering, needs, joys of the other one's own. And our neighbour, loved in this way, almost always responds to our love. To love your enemy, turning him the other cheek, disconcerts him and often turns him into a friend, who in his turn, sets out to love. That's how the Movement grows.

But every element of the structure of the Movement is a way of expressing what it is. The focolare, for example, is a community made up of persons of different callings, nationalities and customs, but all differences are lost in that unity, which invites Jesus and makes him present among them. It is Jesus himself who bears witness and who brings conviction.

It is the same for the groups of volunteers, which are real temporary focolares, for the gen units, for the clergy houses, for the religious communities, for the families renewed by that spirit, or for the Mariapolis where thousands of members of the Movement gather for a few days holiday with only one rule—to make mutual love the basis of their lives.

And it is true of the permanent Mariapolis, like Loppiano near Florence, to which tens of thousands of people travel like modern pilgrims.

I must include the various activities of the young people in the Movement, in particular the "Genfests", where the Gospel message is passed on by the sharing of personal or collective experiences, expressed by means of music, theatre or dance. The music groups, which have come into being in recent times, can be found all over the world, wherever the Movement has reached a certain maturity. The effect of these activities is surprising, because today, young people are searching, often in vain, for something worth dedicating their lives to. We must not forget the press. Magazines have come into existence in the main Western and Eastern languages. Some are still in their infancy, but rich in content, and the publishing houses are producing books on spirituality and religious experience and teaching.

How do members of your community live?

The members of the focolari or the members of the Movement?

I was meaning all the members of the Movement. But since you have corrected me, perhaps it would be a good idea to explain in greater detail the structure of the Movement, which is rather complex, and in which one can easily get lost.

What does the Movement ask of people?—A conversion! It asks that of everyone. It asks us to choose God, to give him his place, the first place in our lives, and that all other values should derive from that choice. We love our parents for obvious reasons, but the deepest reason is that God commands us to do so. We love all men because that is what God wants. It is God who must come first.

Often he is not given the first place. And remember, we ourselves at the start all had other ideals. In my naivety, I had staked everything on philosophy, in the hope of arriving at the truth, and I hadn't yet realised that Jesus Christ was Truth incarnate. When I did realise that, I put my textbooks up in the attic.

That was what was asked of me, because Jesus, who asks us to leave behind for him father, mother, fields, asked me to leave my "fields" which consisted of a few books. Others have no books to put up in the attic but they still have something to set aside. There are individuals in the Movement who are called to live out that demand of the Gospel quite literally, really to leave their families and their fields, their studies, their professions, to go and live in little communities; these are the focolarini.

Naturally they are relatively few in number, (about 2,500) because their life has something radical about it which is not for everyone. As I said to you when we were talking about Foco, the focolare is also open to married people who are eagerly seeking perfection and who want to lose themselves in unity and contribute to begetting Christ in the focolare. For it is Christ who is born with the focolare, and then all that is needed is to let him act. It is he who works miracles, he who converts, he who transforms society. It is up to us to bring Christ into the world, to beget him in our midst.

Other members of the Movement, while feeling themselves called basically to the same thing, do not think they have to follow it physically. They leave all in spirit. They give God the first place, but they stay with their families. They continue to work for a living, but no longer idolise their work. God is their ideal, and it is for him that they exercise their professional calling. We call them the "volunteers."

The many priests who live like this have also had, at some time, to be converted and yield to God the first place, which may have been occupied by their priesthood itself. Priesthood is an awesome reality, but it is still subordinate to God.

Religious have welcomed this spirit, which has renewed many spiritual families, both men and women. Unity has not sown confusion but has revived the spirit and the particular charism of the foundation. It has brought the brethren closer to each other and to their superiors. It has explained the rule and illuminated the original vision of the founder.

As for the "Gen", the new generation of the Movement, these are young people for whom God comes first. The law of God is engraved upon their hearts to the point that they go against the current, like living Gospels. They are signs exposed to contradiction in a world grown sick from eroticism, alienating experiences, violence.

At the heart of the Movement then, there is the focolare. How do you define the focolare?

The focolare is a modern community, made up of a small number of people who live in the world and mingle with the world, dress like everyone else and work like their colleagues, but unlike the others they have renounced the world, they have left their native land, their family, their work to give themselves to the cause of unity.

There now exists a rule, drawn up from experience, which gives a structure to their lives and can be adapted to all circumstances. But the rule which is fundamental to their entire existence is that mutual and continual love, which must never be absent, and which makes possible—within the limits of what human beings can do—the presence of Jesus in their midst. That is the focolare. Without the presence of Jesus among its members, the focolare literally ceases to exist.

There follows from this a radical ascesis which demands a readiness to die for one another, sharing the burdens and cares of others and rejoicing at their joy.

And the consequence is a modern, communitarian mystical life which brings the presence of Christ and enlightens members as to what they must do, about what activities to engage in, so that the life of the focolare is contemplation-action. The focolare is a little piece of living Church. It is already Paradise on earth.

What place does the Movement give to the couples belonging to it who make up a group known as "New Families"?

Their contribution is very important, because we see in these couples two people, to each of whom Jesus says: "He who does not leave father, mother, wife, children and lands cannot be my disciple." So we try to make that aspect of the Gospel a reality in their lives also, so that God may have the first place in the soul of the couple and the family become effectively a little

Church, a household Church.

The "New Humanity" Movement seems to witness to the fact that lay people can get thoroughly involved in a new dimension of the Church.

The "New Humanity" Movement tries to bring the spirit of the Gospel into the world of science, the world of art, into the educational sphere, the medical world, everywhere, not only with a view to the conversion of individuals, but to bring the Gospel to bear upon the structures.

I have heard people talking about permanent Mariapolises in Italy, Africa, Argentina, Brazil, and Germany. The first and most extensive of these is at Loppiano, near Florence.

The permanent Mariapolises aim to be "cities built on a hill." There people live the Gospel and prove from experience that Jesus keeps his promises. For example, "Give and it will be given to you" is a daily experience. And "victory over the world" is likewise a daily experience. At Loppiano there are young people from all over, who are—let's put it plainly—handsome boys and beautiful girls. On Sundays thousands of people come to visit them, but there is no danger that they will be contaminated by the world.

At Loppiano, as in the other permanent Mariapolises, the truth of the Gospel is a matter of experience. For example: "That all may be one, so that the world may believe." They are one, and many visitors rediscover their faith. I know that people approaching Loppiano ask: "Can you point me the way to the village where people live the Gospel?" These villages enable us to say: "Come and see."

Loppiano is also the place where the young focolarini are trained. When they return to their own countries they take with them a picture of how the world ought to be.

When the idea of building Loppiano was born (restoring some old farms and putting up some new buildings), we thought of a college of religion linked to small enterprises, where the young people could work to provide for their needs. Now there are five hundred inhabitants, and Loppiano seems well adapted to Europe, which is where most of the inhabitants and visitors come from. Sound theological teaching, theology informed by Wisdom, is offered to the young people, who come from nations agitated by a whirlwind of ideas.

The Mariapolis near Buenos Aires is engaged in teaching trades. It teaches land cultivation in a region where social problems are particularly acute.

The one at Recife in North-East Brazil has a ministry to people engaged in handcrafts and cottage industries. There has been a progressive influx of the inhabitants of the *mocambos*, which are like shanty-towns built on the unhealthy swamps, with whom we have been living in order to give them a sense of their dignity as men and as Christians.

The Mariapolis at Ottmaring in Germany is ecumenical, for it came into being around a Centre where Catholics and Lutherans share a common life.

You have spoken of the young people. The Movement attracts them; how do you explain their interest?

Young people are generous. They are not afraid of death, perhaps because they have not yet had the time to become attached to the earth. They are idealists by nature. When they are brought face to face with the life of the Gospel and they discover the demands that it involves, they plunge in with enthusiasm. They discover the fatherly love of God and they feel at ease, because even though they will not admit it, they need protection.

The Gospel has a special affinity with the young, because the Gospel is always young.

III
THEY HAVE ENLARGED MY SOUL

You have succeeded in drawing thousands of people into your programme for christian living. Do you think it is possible to bring all the peoples of the Earth together in peace?

Jesus is Peace, and we must have the courage to reject all other methods, all other means and spread the Gospel, because that's where God speaks, where God made man speaks. With the word of God lived and brought to others, what has been realised in the Movement can be spread in the world. It can be done. You see at the beginning we thought we were just leading an ordinary christian life and in a sense that was true. We had no intention of making innovations; we wanted to read the Gospel and live it.

Years later we noticed that the Lord had underlined for us some words in the Gospel which were most relevant to the present time; words which pointed not to individualism but to a spirituality of community. Unity, the testament of Jesus, his last prayer addressed to the Father, where he asks that all may be one had become the charter of the Movement.

"That all may be one." So you are thinking of all men without exception, even if it has to begin with "two or three."

That expression "two or three" had brought us to love our brothers and sisters but also our enemies in order to build bridges to everyone. In an even more special way it made us understand the words which create community, and which urge upon us the living of a communitarian spiritual life.

That is why I believe I can say that the Movement offers a Gospel for this age.

This programme of unity which the Gospel puts forward, is it really perceived as such by the men of today? Has the Christian message not lost a good part of its credibility because of the fact that, rightly or wrongly, it has become assimilated into western culture, indeed to western colonialism?

The world of today is no longer the same as in earlier times; it is in the process of understanding itself retrospectively through the means of social communication. Radio, newspapers, and above all television are beginning to introduce us to peoples and religions which were totally unknown to us.

We are in an age where it is necessary to acquire a way of thinking which is not only Western, Moslem, Buddhist or Oriental. We must acquire a mentality which is truly universal in its scope.

The meeting which has taken place between the peoples and civilisations of the whole world is irreversible by now because of the explosion in the means of communication and the tremendous development of technology. That encounter has certainly been enriching, because it has brought an exchange of news, knowledge, facts, events, traditions, ways of thinking, making everything common property and exploding in every man cultural and national ideas which he had lived with up till then. The encounter has been very enriching, since among other things it has made it obvious how these opinions often did not correspond to the truth, but were completely one-sided because they were the result of a lack of communication among different peoples. You only need to think how the same historical facts were, and still are even now, seen and taught in different countries, often in a completely contradictory way. For example an individual whom one nation considers a hero is often seen as a traitor in another country. And a period of history which thinkers illuminated by the higher truth of the faith have considered a golden age, one of great illumination, is seen as a dark age by others who are guided only by the light of their own intelligence in willingly making an abstraction out of God.

Today no-one can still accept these biased and contradictory perceptions.

If the break with old ways of seeing things has had any merit it has been that of unmasking many falsities in a sincere desire to know the pure truth beyond different human interpretations.

So this world-wide communion has been, and is, a good thing?

Yes, but there is the other side of the coin. In reality, it's only now that we can grasp the different ways of thinking of different peoples, because we are only now beginning to approach these people other than as colonisers who consider their way of seeing the world and life as the only right and valid one; we are beginning to approach these peoples with the respect which is due to them, with the humility of the one who knows he has always something to learn. And thus we perceive that there is another way of seeing the same things which is quite different from our Western way, but which is no less true and valid. In effect we have all been schooled more or less by the disciplines of Greek and Roman thinking. Socrates, Plato, Aristotle, Cicero have taught us how to think. The language, the vocabulary that we use have been in great measure shaped by them. Moreover at the present time technology is dominant in our culture. And we are faced with peoples who know nothing of Greece, of Rome or our way of thinking but whose great civilisations are founded on other names, other thinkers, also very great, and who are completely unknown to us.

What is happening then?

We are realising that our mental structure, our way of thinking is not the only one, is not unique. This discovery, especially if it happens repeatedly can have an effect on the Westerner and leave him perplexed. It is as if he were to discover that he had in his head a crystal through which he saw everything, and that that crystal was in the process of breaking up.

Our concepts, our traditions, our ways of thinking confronted more and more often with other traditions and turns of mind are no longer managing to resist. The entire human race is experiencing a greater or lesser degree of uncertainty and suffering which will become more and more severe as that encounter between peoples who have hitherto been apart, spreads to different parts of the world.

And why is that?

Because the structure of the Western mind is so bound to the absolute values that it contains and expresses, like ethics, aesthetics, metaphysics, liberty, justice, that you can think that these values themselves have been compromised.

Are you saying that the ever more extensive use of the means of communication is threatening not only to produce a crisis in what was partial, but to arouse fears in men unprepared for such a thing that the great values might waver in which former generations had always firmly believed?

That is not all. In the domain of religion, the man who possesses a child-like faith (that is, a faith not reinforced by a deeper study and above all by a deep personal experience of that absolute truth which lives at the centre of his soul and manifests itself to whoever puts it into practice) may also find himself disoriented, uncertain of what he believes. In effect, the Church, which bears the transcendant and absolute truth—the universal Church by vocation and in fact—has often had to employ, in order to express itself and make itself understood, the language, vocabulary and thought patterns characteristic of the world in which it has developed. And many have thought that these expressions contained the totality of the truth that the Church has to offer. The fact is that human absolute truths and values, like revealed truth must on no account be confused with our mental structures, which contain them like an envelope. The vacillation in the Western mode of thought and the distrust which one may have of it ought not, must not, give the impression that these absolute values themselves are compromised.

The truth is so tied to the thought which expresses it that they might be thought inseparable.

It is not so by any means. Yet in this new situation which has arrived little by little, uncertainty exists, unease is growing and in the midst of such an ideological earthquake men are trying to find shelter in all kinds of ways.
There are those who, in fear, cling to the culture they have learnt and want to die in peace, leaving to future generations the task of finding the solution to such a problem.

There are those who only take account of human strength and embark on a quest for new civilisations, new ideas and, also, other religions, presuming to find a satisfactory synthesis. That group often falls into a hybrid syncretism where the absolute truth becomes relative and the other truths they discover vary according to their mood, their character, what they find agreeable. A mixture of notions springs from that, in which there is nothing left that is solid, valid, absolute, and which falls into the most absurd relativism and the most varied subjectivism.

There are those who want to hasten the destruction of the old world, as if the end of one world that has been superseded must bring about the birth of a new one.

And there are yet others who cannot be bothered thinking about it all and who throw themselves into a blind pragmatism, leaving to others the effort of producing a new world.

The young person who cannot hide from reality and who also feels all that himself, very often has the intuition that the earth is shaking under his feet.

And, moreover, he can no longer cling to a purely Western mode of thought; for since he is young he has not yet assimilated the mentality of the preceding generation. So he has a further cause for suffering and entering consciously into giving birth to the new world. All the more so since he is responsible for it; he cannot close his eyes and avoid sharing in the birth-pangs of this world which, tomorrow, will belong to him.

How then can we live in this terrible world of today when, by a mysterious cataclysm the highest values are rocking on their foundations like enormous sky-scrapers swaying and collapsing?

One means exists that we can count on to contribute to bringing the new world into being. There exists a kind of world-man who feels, who has felt in himself that terrible tidal wave which threatens to save nothing of what had hitherto been held beyond discussion; and who, whilst fearing almost that absolute truth itself was abandoning him to his fate, throwing him into the gravest confusion, was yet able at the same time to withstand so enormous a trial, thus paying for a new world which he found in himself and brought into being for others. Yes, he exists. But suddenly you realise that this man cannot just be a man, but that he must be the Man. It is Jesus crucified and forsaken.

His perfect humanity, though frail and subject to pain and death, is the symbol of all human structures which despite their limitations have succeeded in containing, in different circumstances, something infinite, like absolute human truths and the supernatural truth which is the kingdom of God.

On the cross, at the gates of physical death, and in the abandonment, his mystical death, Jesus felt the collapse of his whole humanity, of his human frame. And at the very depths of that collapse the Father mysteriously allowed him to doubt the presence of God in him, almost as if it had vanished. That's why he cried, "My God, my God, why have you forsaken me?"

But in this very cry, Jesus, because he is God, had the strength to overcome that infinite agony. And he gave to his mortal flesh the power of immortality by taking it up, resurrected, into the heart of the immortal Trinity.

This really is a new vision of the Cross!

That's not all, for with that phenomenal acceptance of the most terrible destruction that heaven and earth have ever known, Jesus gives mankind the possibility, on the one hand, of rising to the life beyond by the resurrection of the body, and, on the other hand, of overcoming spiritually in this life any death, any destruction in which man may find himself.

Just as, after his abandonment in Calvary he poured out the Holy Spirit on the apostles, so to those who love him and follow him he offers the Spirit of Truth.

As we follow him we will find the possibility of not trembling before any situation but on the contrary, confronting it in the certainty that all human truth, and the kingdom of God which is the Truth, will be able to find new mental structures at the world's level.

That idea is really fascinating, almost too good to be true.

We must not draw back before the boldness of certain ideas. With someone who has vanquished death, we can aspire to inaccessible goals.

In 1977 you were awarded the Templeton Prize for Progress in Religion. What were your feelings when you learned of that honour?

At the time I was upset. Why on earth a prize for religion? I had always thought it was Paradise which rewarded your love of God and your brother. Then I felt a certain annoyance. I said to myself: "This is deflecting me from my course. The Gospel has taught me that the left hand must not know what the right hand is doing." The idea of that publicity troubled me deeply. But the Gospel itself reassured me: "Let men see your good works and give glory to the Father." I am very conscious that the Focolare Movement is not my business but God's. I have only been an instrument in his hand. The Movement gives off a light which comes from God. That light must not be hidden under a bushel but placed on the lampstand so that it gives light to all those in the house, and thus to everyone. Then I said to myself: "If the Templeton Prize serves to glorify God, let them give it to me." Having said that I felt a little personal surge of joy, the joy of a schoolgirl who has been given a good mark and is pleased not only for herself but for her mother. They could have chosen a person from another religion, but that year they chose a Catholic. That made me happy for the Catholic Church, my mother.

If you think back to your stay in London for the giving of the prize, what memories of it have you kept?

Outwardly, those might be reckoned extraordinary days. But from my point of view there is nothing extraordinary except the love of God. If my companions and I lived those moments whilst loving God, then they were extraordinary. But if at the culminating moments we failed to love God then we fell back into the flattest banality.

Be that as it may, I can sum up those days in a single impression. It seems to me that the Lord used that occasion to open the Movement to another horizon. We already had friendly relations with the faithful of other religions in Hong Kong, Korea and Japan for example. But that day in London, the contact was immediate and rather exceptional. After my address at the Guildhall in front of representatives of many religions, I had the impression that we were all one, as if the will of Jesus had been realised.

I think it is because we all believed in God; perhaps at that moment he enveloped us all. I was very moved to see that the quickest to come and congratulate me were in fact the faithful of other religions. The first was a Lama who came up to me and said that he was writing to the Dalai Lama to suggest that he got in touch with me. Then four Jews explained to me with great joy that the Bible was the vine on which the Gospel was grafted. I had the feeling that they wanted me to understand that the Movement also found its origins in the Bible. They were so friendly that you could have thought that unity had already been achieved.

After them three Indians, members of the Sikh religion, came forward. The Sikhs are a movement which has spread extensively in Asia and whose founder lived in the 15th century. They described to me their efforts to bring Hinduism and Islam together, thinking that would please me, since they also were working for the unity of the religions.

That immediate encounter with brothers of other religions quite threw me and showed me the will of God. From now on we were not only to spread this spirit, this love, this life among the churches and Christian communities but to turn frankly towards our brothers and sisters in the other religions to see what was the Lord's plan. I did not know where he would lead us. I knew nothing more. What I knew was that I had found myself at ease there, I was understood by them and I understood them.

How might we get past the differences in faith, doctrine and mentality and approach unity?

There is only one way: love. But love must never have strings attached, or it ceases to be love. If we love in order to win people over to God we achieve nothing. If we really love, we will talk about the rain perhaps, or the fine weather and the other person will confide his anxieties to us, he will tell us about everything that interests him and we will make ourselves one with him. When the conversation is over, the other will go away and we will perhaps again be tempted to say to ourselves; "What a pity! That was a waste of time! Will

I ever have the chance of seeing him again?" But that's getting it wrong. Now we must love the next person we meet, even it it's a friend, a lifelong companion.

Then we will understand that love is never without consequence. A day will come when someone will ask us how we live. We may have to wait years but what does that matter? It is better to take the time to sow seed if in the end a plant is to grow.

The moment will have come to put forward, as well as the other points of our spirituality, the word of life. We will say how, month after month we live a word of the Gospel to re-evangelise ourselves and we will recount our experiences of the word we are living that month.

They also will want to live some equivalent of the word of life and they will go and look in the Koran, for example, for a word analogous to ours and they will live it among themselves. They will study the Koran more deeply. They will live it and they will get to know at the same time our word of life. A dialogue of life and experience will be established. They will tell us their experiences and we will tell them ours. We will go forward together, we in Christianity, they in their religion. The more we advance and the more we are united to God, the more God definitely blesses and enlightens.... And the Gospel penetrates into their community and quickens it with life.

Where the Buddhists are concerned, I have got to know the leaders of a Buddhist movement, the Rissho Kosei-Kai and its founder, Mr. Nikkyo Niwano.

He was the first and only Non-Christian observer at the Second Vatican Council.

He is a wise man, attentive to the spirit, sensitive to the supernatural, humble and able to appreciate good wherever it may be found. His fellow workers are very hospitable, courteous, open. Members of the Rissho Kosei-Kai, especially young people accompanied by their leaders have expressed a desire to know about our faith, touched, I believe, by the witness of mutual love and particularly attracted by Mary. This interest in the Virgin gives us great reason for hope. We have embarked upon a stable and constructive dialogue with them.

In the sixties the Movement began to make contact with the other Christian confessions. Do you remember your first intuition of the way ahead on the ecumenical front?

I was in Darmstadt in Germany in a community of Lutheran women religious, and at their request I was speaking about our spirituality. In the audience there were three quite well-known pastors. At the end, their comments surprised me: "What? Are Catholics living the Gospel?" From that moment on the bond between us became stronger. They asked us to bring this spirit into their community and into the Lutheran church generally. And in Germany now wherever the Focolare Movement exists it is to be found also among the Lutherans. We share as much as is possible. In the course of the years we have seen many prejudices disappear on both sides. That was the point of departure for our ecumenism which then spread to the Anglicans, the Reformed Churches, the Orthodox, etc.

What aspects of spirituality interested them particularly?

The other day, a boy who had come to a meeting organised by the young people, went away saying: "God is love and you have made him visible for me." Probably he noticed the unity of these young people and saw—with the sixth sense which the soul possesses—someone among them, God, made present by mutual love.

Basically, when you accept the God of Love, implicitly you are accepting the whole of Revelation and all the Christian faith. And there is a breach made in the dividing wall which separates the Christian denominations and even the different religions.

You have met the greatest ecumenical personalities of our times. What do you retain from these encounters?

They have enlarged my soul with the knowledge of all the riches which exist outside the Catholic Church.

I have kept a strong impression of my numerous meetings with Patriarch Athenagoras. He was a man of exceptional stature, both humanly and in the things of the spirit.

I remember my first visit. I had told him how I wanted to work for the unity of Christians and also for the unity of the different nations. And he said to me: "You are my daughter. You have two fathers. One big father in Rome, Paul II. Yes you know, he's a second Saint Paul, not Paul VI at all—and then an old father here." He spoke to me about Paul VI in a way unlike anything I have ever heard.

He had a love for him which showed itself in great occasions and in little details. For example, he would ask me: "Are you sure he's eating enough? Is he getting out for a walk? Is he getting some fresh air. . . ?"

He always read the *L'Osservatore Romano* and he knew all the Pope's speeches. Everything the Pope did, he used to say he was doing it with him. He confided to me: "You know, I live in a tiny little room, right next to the Pope's office." And when the Pope was on his travels abroad, he would tell me: "I went to such and such a country with the Pope, and then we went to such and such a place," and so on. And for him these "travels" were in a way more real than his enforced confinement at Istanbul because his closeness to the Pope was spiritual, supernatural, and thus more real than geographical distance.

Athenagoras taught me not only that love of the Pope, but also the charity which puts actions before words.

He never let me start a serious conversation before I had accepted something from him (a *loukom* or some coffee). He would make sure that the hotel was paid by himself, for as his guest I was to pay for nothing. He would have me stay to lunch with him, although the *Phanar* was a kind of monastery but he had installed a little room for visitors where I could have my meal.

And since the rule imposed numerous days of fasting and abstinence so that I shouldn't suffer, he most considerately ordered some caviar.

But he also achieved great things. He had a great love for all the different peoples. In the course of a long life he had got to know many of them and I was impressed to see how he valued the beauty of each one. I don't know how he did it. I think he had a gift for that. He taught me to love the different nations, to find good in them all. I never heard him speak evil of anyone. Athenagoras was truly great, I will never forget him.

He opened my eyes to the Orthodox Church and its immense riches which go back to the first Fathers of the Church. I became aware in particular of its sense of Christian charity and faith as a way of life, to say nothing of its splendid liturgy.

Athenagoras incarnated Orthodoxy, the beauty of Orthodoxy but he was already spiritually one with the Catholic Church

You also met the Prior of Taizé.

I could say a lot about that but I'll limit myself to one detail. I have always been struck by the way his face glows with light. A light unlike any other. The light of God.

You also know the personalities of the Lutheran world.

Once I went to Münich to visit the then President of the Lutheran Federation, Dr. Dietzfelbinger. At that time I was just beginning to learn how to be involved in ecumenism, and I remember that at one point I found myself, a little embarrassed, under a large portrait of Luther! But then I saw the fine open face of that bishop and I felt at ease. I talked of my experience as a Catholic trying to live her faith. Naturally I did not sidestep what was characteristic of Catholicism, the place that the Pope held for me, the obedience I considered due to the bishops. After I had described my work and opened up my ideas, I had the feeling that he was in agreement with everything because I had referred back to the Gospel throughout and, as a good Lutheran, he loved the Gospel.

After this first contact, relationships developed and it was he who, in agreement with the Catholic bishop, encouraged the establishment of an Ecumenical Centre at Augsburg, the very place where, in the sixteenth century, relations between Lutherans and Catholics had broken down.

Can you say something about the members of the World Council of Churches?

When I met them, I felt I was meeting brothers and sisters with whom we were engaged in a struggle for the same cause, fighting with different weapons, taking different routes, sometimes with a different perspective but in every case with a view to the union of the Church.

And how do you now see the Catholic Church?

Since 1960 my experience has been ecumenical. But I must say the effect of that experience has been to reinforce more and more my confidence in the Catholic Church. And I say this openly without fear of offending my friends in the other denominations, for I know that they hold the Focolare Movement in high regard precisely because it has avoided compromise and has always said what it believed to be the truth, in complete unity with the Catholic Church.

After a first interview with Dr. Ramsey in 1966, and later with Dr. Coggan, you met the present Primate of the Church of England, Dr. Runcie, in 1981. How would you evaluate the relations between the Anglican communion and the Roman Catholic Church? Will we have long to wait for re-union?

It will take a certain number of years. In ecumenical activity people often want to speed things up and at the beginning that was my desire also. Today I think that if no-one makes a start no-one will finish either. So let's be happy to be among those who are making a start; tomorrow others can finish the work. But I don't feel that we'll have to wait long for the Anglican Church because it seems to me that the Holy Spirit is really at work.

Let's return if you will to your meetings with the Patriarch Athenagoras. He had set himself a great objective: the one chalice. You yourself have reported him as saying: "The day will come when the sun will be high in the sky and the angels dancing and singing; and we, bishops and patriarchs, we will be gathered round the Pope and we will celebrate the one chalice."

It was his favourite theme, the summit of his reflections. He said to me one day: "I am living out our times to the full. This age is the demonstration of God's goodness. I can't understand how we have got this far after nine centuries of living in separation. How can God have given us this joy, this hope?" The last time I met him he added: "It will be like a day in Paradise for me when I go back to Rome and see the Pope again and conclude with that event." (He was alluding to the one chalice.) And he explained: "Yes we are working, and we are asking the good God to help us to take these steps. The theologians are not in a position to resolve these questions and they are important ones. It is sad to be having theological discussions about things which belong to each Church like a particular treasure. For example, we cannot ask the Pope to abandon infallibility and primacy. Everything that belongs to him is part of the riches of the Church and we also in our Churches have something special."

What do you see as the function of the Movement in this work of unification?

Right from the beginning we were aware of a convergence of thoughts, feelings and methods. Athenagoras put his confidence above all in the "dialogue of love" rather than in theological dialogue and he saw in the Movement a way of realising this dialogue of love. Also from the very first moment he demonstrated a moving confidence in us and a warm affection because he saw that our ecumenism was made of life, of the communion of souls. He even formed the habit of calling himself, with a smile, a "simple member" of the Movement, and he used to say: "We all need this spirit."

We are convinced that the dialogue with him has not been cut off by his death and the way he has opened must be pursued.

What does that way consist of exactly?

We already have something which unites us, or which at least can unite us; it is the presence of Jesus in our midst. We are all baptised; Jesus can be in our midst if we love one another as he has loved us, being ready to die for one another.

How would you assess the present state of ecumenism given the experience that you have of it?

I think of a bottle which you can call either half empty or half full. Before I began to work for ecumenism I grieved at what was missing. Now I am full of wonder and gratitude to God who has preserved in the Churches such riches of faith, hope and charity; there the understanding of prayer, here liturgy, elsewhere, the value of the word of God. I have come to appreciate that we are a single family of nearly a billion Christians, even if something—very little at times—

is holding back the full unification of the various Churches.

We are all brothers and sisters who love Christ, at least, who strive to love him. To have this common denominator is already a lot.

If the division of Christians into hundreds of denominations can produce a feeling of vertigo, especially in someone who reflects on the problems posed by their re-unification, when you are immersed in work among these brothers and sisters and you love them, you experience a quite special kind of joy. This is not just a way of talking. It is a joy that you experience nowhere else: it is rediscovering yourselves as brothers and sisters because Christ is present in each one. Right away you are impelled to draw the consequences, and to put in common and share all the spiritual goods. Love works miracles and raises up in all the Churches people devoted to unity who work at the heart of their own Church, loving, enlightening, spending themselves, but all to arrive at one end: a single Church.

Do you think we will all fit together easily into one Church?

It has to be. One shepherd, one flock. Obviously it has to be. We will have to see how that one Church will be put together. I suppose the Holy Spirit will preserve numerous traditions that we have, many customs, rites of the different Churches, but there will be unity, without any doubt. There will be unity in charity and in faith.

The fact that several denominations exist keeps the whole more alive. If unity is realised do we not risk losing that vitality?

Divisions are always pernicious, but when people begin to love God with sincerity, everything works together for good, and thus tomorrow when we are one, we shall be enriched by the variety of customs, ways of thinking and also by the diversity of interpretation of the same truth in which we believe in the same way, with the same faith.

So everyone can keep his individuality?

Lost in unity.

It's very important what you are saying.

It is important. If unity is guaranteed it is a good thing that everyone should maintain his own individuality. The Catholic Church itself is made like that; it is one but it is composed of numerous local Churches in which however the whole Church lives. Every local Church has its characteristics. For example, the Church in Africa is very different from the Church in England or the Church in Argentina. Pluralism is inherent in unity. What could you unite, if not that which is different? Uniting like with like makes no sense. The important thing is that there should be the one faith, expressed in this variety of ways.

Serious work for ecumenism has been undertaken by the experts and theologians in the joint commissions and other conferences. What can be the contribution of lay people to this search for unity?

Above all, lay people can pray, and here, prayer is more than necessary because the undertaking is not a simple one. We have to make good centuries of disunity, indifference, etc. So we need a helping hand from Heaven. But if ecumenism is to succeed, if its results are to be lasting, the consent of the people is necessary and the vast majority of the people are laity. In the past other ecumenical initiatives have been abortive because they have failed to gain consent. Now the laity can do much to ensure that the Church feels itself to be one and that this feeling remains strong after the re-union of the Churches. Education for unity is needed.

Lay people can help to bring about that education for unity by keeping up a strong flow of mutual love among Christians who historically have been separated. In order to feel ourselves to be one we must understand each other, and if we want to understand each other we must love each other. We have already received and thanks to theological dialogue we will, as time goes on, receive more and more documents drawn up by joint commissions which address themselves to the problems of the faith. They must be circulated so that our understanding of each other may deepen. But sometimes these documents are written in a style which is not easily understood and yet lay people must be able to explain them to other lay people. This is a piece of groundwork at grassroots level, which is very useful, even indispensable.

IV
THE SPIRITUALITY OF UNITY

In the course of these discussions a word that you have frequently returned to is "spirituality." It's a word that at one and same time attracts and repells because of the different pictures it evokes. What exactly do you mean by "spirituality?"

I like to go back to a definition given in our own times by Cardinal Montini: "A spirituality is a way of realising the ideal of the Christian life." A spirituality is a life or rather the Life—Christianity, the Gospel—seen from a particular angle.

So it concerns every dimension of a man's existence. You would not limit it to devotion with the undertones of sentimentalism that that implies?

Of course not. The Christian is a new person. The old person is dead, or at least he is mastered by Life, which is Christ living in the Christian. But you cannot become a new person without accepting the message of Christ in its totality.

A Christianity which confined itself to the regeneration of the moral and spiritual life of the individual according to an evangelical code would be a nonsense.

It would have emptied the Gospel of a good part of its substance and especially loving the other "as" oneself. An authentic Christianity is by nature oriented to community. Even the Christianity of the hermit in so far as he does not live for himself but for the Church is one of community. The Christian life inevitably reflects the life of the Trinity, in which there are three Persons. If Christianity is lived like that, if it is the Gospel lived, the new person is new in everything because he is directed from within by the Spirit of Christ who "renews the face of the earth."

If we deplore the fact that Christianity does not sufficiently influence every aspect of human life, let us say straight away that it is not the Christianity that Christ wanted. The new person is another Christ, and just as the historical Christ revolutionised his world, another Christ cannot but revolutionise his one. As for the danger of sentimentalism which you mentioned, I would reply that the heart is part and parcel of every stage in the spiritual life, but a little experience of the love of God enables us to distinguish sentimentalism immediately and not to overestimate our feelings, even the most exalted of them. The secret is to learn to lose everything in order to begin loving God again with one's will. With time, as it acquires the habit of returning to God in all the countless vicissitudes of life, the heart eventually is captivated by God and you feel that it is he whom you love above all else. It seems to me that this is a precious conquest in the spiritual life, since it is the best preparation for the crossing over to real life where we will be alone with him.

Having got thus far, while continuing to love everyone you love him above all and find yourself ready in all simplicity to lose the others, in order to possess only him—but it takes years of faithfulness and the help of God to get to that stage.

Let's go back to the spirituality of unity. The Movement then, considers the Gospel from the point of view of unity.

As I have said, from the first days, I have been strongly drawn by the last prayer of Jesus to the Father and I thought at once that the objective which the Lord had in mind for us was to work within the Church for the unity of the human family.

It was Jesus who prayed to the Father and we think that his prayer cannot have gone unheard. The Movement has placed itself in the hands of God so that he can use it in order to realise in the Church and with the Church, the ardent desire expressed by his Son on the eve of his death.

From the point of view of unity, what do you stress particularly in the Gospel?

Our spirituality is all the Gospel. That conviction has been with us from the beginning. And you could say that it was the translation of the Gospel into our lives that unleashed the little revolution in Trent which you have heard about. The mentality of Jesus and his ways of doing things took the place of our own, to the great scandal of those watching. As for ourselves, we were intending, quite innocently, to live the Gospel, the Gospel of all times, the Gospel of everyone. Unknown to us God, as you were saying, was engraving on our hearts a few words which have remained the directing force of our spirituality. All these words were given to us in the first months, although it would be true to say that the understanding we have of them is greater today.

At the beginning of these discussions you said that your first great discovery was that the love of God conquers all. Is that not the first of these leading ideas on which your spirituality is built?

It is difficult to imagine the reversal produced by that truth understood in a completely new way. Our Christian life even though it was accompanied by coherent practice and solid faith appeared grey and sickly in that brilliant light: God is love, God is Father. He is not an inactive God in his distant heaven. Our hearts which have suffered exile, come out of the darknesss and are united to him who loves us and watches over us.

Our circumstances, both happy and painful take on a meaning because all is foreseen by the love of God. Nothing can scare us any more or take away our peace. Our eyes see differently. God is behind everything that concerns us. We feel understood, known, personally loved. We are "in God's hand" and nothing can happen to us without his agreement.

You have chosen God as the ideal of your life and following your example hundreds of thousands of men and women have found him again and chosen him. This is surprising when you consider the present critical state of religious faith.

We have not chosen God: God has chosen us. It is he who has made himself known in his beauty, his charm, his tenderness, his truth. He has made himself known above all by his Gospel of which we have had to admit the truth. He has never let us down. His promises have been fulfilled. He said: "Give and it will be given to you." We have to say that he has never been outdone in generosity. He said: "If you are united in my name, ask and you will receive." Our prayers have always been answered.

He promised the conversion of those around us if we are united in his name. We have seen thousands converted.

The beatitudes have shown themselves to be true. Jesus said that he is the way, the truth and the life; it is true. Following him, you go forward to the goal, every question finds its answer, even suffering, even death. You feel the life of God stirring within you, that spiritual life of which the birth and development through successive stages are described by the Gospel.

How could we fail to love him who fills our lives, making them dynamic and fruitful? Him who nourishes our lives so that they do not perish but open into eternity?

When you have found out that everything Jesus says is true, it is easy to leave any other master. In our times people like to go by their experiences. Now the Gospel is there at hand. It speaks to us of the fire which Jesus lights in the loving heart and which blazes away in us. How could we not love such a man? If anyone does not believe in his divinity let him put the Gospel to the test, simply and without prejudice, and he will be convinced that this man can be none other than God. That is what is so attractive about this life: its divinity. It is there, silently entering the hearts of men; while the world wears the mask of atheism it is there, preparing a revolution which will one day burst forth, stronger than ever. Yes, because there is another true word in the Gospel: "Have no fear, I have overcome the world."

God loves us first, he chooses us, and we respond, more or less, to his love by choosing him ourselves and in trying to love him in our neighbour. There are so many good works to do, we feel the call to respond to so many situations of need, and often the different responses seem contradictory. We were speaking of the risk of religious sentimentality; there is also the risk of activism, which is perhaps even more serious. How and where do we begin?

Faith in the love which God has for us, has impelled us to apply the words of the Gospel which tell us how we can respond to that love with our love. It is at this point that a verse keeps coming into our minds: "It is not he who says to me 'Lord, Lord,' who will enter into the kingdom of Heaven but he who does the will of my father." Loving consists in doing the will of God.

Talk of the will of God can easily suggest an idea of resignation or fatalism.

On the contrary, it is the most fantastic adventure that can be given to a man to live. He does not follow his own mediocre will: he gives up the attempt to achieve his limited projects in order to abandon himself to God and realise the plan that he has for his son, a divine plan, beyond description, very rich.

In order to respond with love to the love of God, we must do his will, but we often have the feeling of just plodding along without seeing any results; how should we set about obtaining the best "results"?

The secret consists in doing the will of God in the present (since the past is past and the future does not depend on us) and living it to perfection, with solemnity.

The will of God is the pearl of great price in the parable. It is a way of perfection, open to all because it can be lived no matter where, in no matter what circumstances, and whatever a person's particular vocation may be.

How can we know the will of God? It is not always apparent.

We must be in a state of recollection, having freed ourselves of things that condition us, of agitation, noise, the confused ideas which fill our heads and the egoism of our daily lives which stifles impulses to improvement.

We must live within, listening always to the voice which speaks in us; conscience, the voice of God—it amounts to the same thing—and then act in accordance with that voice until the day comes when we are incapable of an outward action if we are not in agreement within. There is something in us which maintains contact with the inside, with the way of God, with his will.

And if the contact is broken? What if our inner lives go into a skid and we feel we are swerving out of control?

Then we will return within and get into touch again with Jesus. We will say to him, "I want to do everything for you according to your word and I am joining myself to you in unity again," and we will go forward in complete tranquillity of spirit.

Our inner life in union with God will ripen progressively until it reaches the state that the mystics call "passivity".

But that is not passivity in the sense of inaction or insensibility.

No. It means simply that God guides the soul himself.

And what becomes of human freedom in that case?

When you love, you feel your freedom developing precisely when you are acting according to the desires of the person who you love. So you reach true freedom if you do the will of God.

You feel a very pure, spiritual joy when you become aware of having been set free from everything that kept your inner life in bondage. It is a liberation above all from yourself, from your will, your schemes, your prejudices, a liberation also from other people and from things. You are free from everything and nothing and no-one has a pull on you.

And what if someone uses your good will as a chance to stab you in the back?

That will still happen of course, but you are free. Even in the depths of a prison you are free, when you have elected to adapt yourself to the circumstances which God has presented to you. You have chosen to love friend and foe alike, to welcome both good luck and ill-fortune because the one just as much as the other can be the manifestation of the will of God who is love. And when you want what God wants you are free.

Loving one's enemies is a feature of the Gospel message. But is it really realistic? You can attract enmity precisely because you are trying to live without compromise and that is seen as a provocation.

Love for your enemy must be doubled. It is not I who am saying that, but the Gospel: "If someone should strike you on the right cheek, offer him also the left." We must love our friends and then love our enemies twice as much. If we love them well and every hurtful word, every barbed remark is taken as a caress and we lose none of our calm, the "enemies" will give up bothering us because their attempts to humiliate us are baffled. So a double portion of love for them.

Loving God, loving one's neighbour. These two commandments are in theory only one but, in practice, you can hesitate over how you ought to proceed. If for example you are at prayer and someone turns up, must you interrupt your prayer in order to offer help to another person, or does God automatically come before other people unless it is someone who demands absolute priority?

It is all a matter of doing the will of God at every instant of the day. Then we can be assured of loving God and our neighbour even if in some particular case we are only attending directly to one of the two. Sometimes the will of God is clearly that we should pray, for example on Sunday at Mass. If another person asks us to do something for him at that time we should explain truthfully that we will be otherwise engaged. We will put as much love as possible into our words and our attitude to soften the disappointment caused by a temporary refusal and we will commit ourselves to giving the help requested a little later.

Conversely it is logical that a grave and urgent necessity can come before prayer. However, we should watch that we do not too readily sacrifice communion with God for the sake of our neighbour. He loves to be loved in our neighbours, but he also desires order in things. In the long term if we do not pray, if we do not cultivate contact with God we will eventually lose interest in others too. Prayer is the breathing of the soul.

Contact with God matures as we cultivate an "inner" life but also as we turn towards others. And if two turn towards each other love becomes mutual. Christian love is not yet completely itself if it is not mutual. Loving one's enemy is not enough; he must become a friend.

In fact Jesus speaks of loving one another as a new commandment, and one which comes from him: "This is my commandment, that you love one another as I have loved you." "There is no greater love than this, that a man should give his life for his friends." This commandment which was the object of a pact concluded among the first focolarini has become, as it were, the connecting tissue of the whole Movement. The simple practice of it produces extraordinary effects. Those who apply it notice a profound change in their inner lives, which are enriched, strengthened, emboldened, and they blossom forth and pick themselves up after every fall. It is no exaggeration to affirm that this is to share in a real conversion which, moreover, is contagious for "all men will know that you are my disciples if you have love for one another." Many find their whole lives change, others hear a call, many gifts of God are bestowed. Mutual love is a reflection of the life of the Trinity such that men can live it.

Linked with the new commandment comes the promise, fundamental to the Movement, of the presence of Christ among those who love each other.

That is true. The new commandment has prepared us for the practice of another fundamental concept which has become, in a sense, obligatory for us: "Where two or three are gathered together in my name, there am I in the midst of them." That is the rule of rules, the premise to every other law, so as to ensure the spiritual presence of Christ among brothers and to give a direction to the brotherhood which Jesus brought on earth for all humanity.

That special presence of Christ among men presumes that at least two people are in agreement. But when you yourself are ready to love, you do not always have at your disposition a partner in the same frame of mind. No doubt in communities constituted like the focolares the rule of rules can be observed with a certain continuity, but the members of the Movement—the focolarini themselves—spend a good part of their day at work for example, in the company of people who do not necessarily share their point of view and are about as eager to have Jesus in their midst as they are to have a run of bad luck.

That does not prevent them from doing their bit by loving, and keeping on loving right to the end. Love is more efficacious and more highly appreciated by God the more disinterested it is , even in respect of spiritual rewards to which we can legitimately aspire, like the presence of Jesus.

All right, we must love; but what does that mean exactly?

Loving someone consists in doing for him what you would like him to do for you. For example if I were in pain I should like to be comforted; if I were in a state of doubt I should like someone to offer me certainty; if I were ignorant I should like someone to instruct me;

if I had nothing to wear I should like someone to give me clothes; if I were ill I should be hoping for a visit; if I were hungry or thirsty I should be glad if someone gave me a meal or drink. Even if I were full of joy I should like someone to share it with, because a joy shared is a joy doubled. To love someone then means doing for others what you would like done for yourself and conversely not doing what you would not like done to you. For example I should not like to be slandered; so I must not slander anyone or abandon them.

But you say that we must love everyone. Are there no exceptions?

It is not enough to love one's relatives or friends. And the motive for loving everyone is that Jesus takes for himself what we do for anyone else on earth. When he met Paul on the road to Damascus, he revealed himself to him in a great light and asked him: "Saul, Saul, why are you persecuting me?" Paul, who was then still called Saul was not persecuting Jesus in person, he was persecuting the Christians but Jesus took for himself what Saul was making the Christians endure. The Gospel also warns us that at the end of our lives we will undergo a kind of examination: "I was hungry," Jesus will say, "and you fed me, I was naked and you clothed me, I was sick and in prison and you visited me" etc. And in our surprise we will question him: "But when can I have done that for you?" And he will reply, "As often as you did it to the least of my brethren, you did it to me." So we must love everyone. It follows that we must love the lovable, and also those whom we find difficult; the beautiful and also the ugly, the great and also the humble, our fellow citizen and also the stranger, a person of our own race, someone who shares our ideas and also someone who thinks differently. We must really love everyone.

But not everyone at once, I take it, not on a global scale but individually, one person after another as he or she becomes our neighbour?

It is essential to have a clear idea of who our neighbour is; he or she is the person next to me in this present moment of my life.

If I understand you correctly, the neighbour is thus a very concrete, flesh and blood individual, who belongs neither to the past nor to the future but to the present. He is here now. We travel on the way of universal love by loving one person at a time.

Jesus gave us an example of this when he washed the feet of his disciples. He was God and he washed our feet, and so we men can also wash the feet of our brothers and sisters. Not just can but must! That's Christianity; serving, serving everyone, seeing everyone as our master. If we are servants, it follows that the others are our masters. Christianity is not a joke, it's not a varnish on the surface of our lives, a little compassion, a little love, a little charitable giving. It is easy to give alms to salve one's conscience and then criticise this one, critcise that one, command, oppress. . . that's too easy.

But what is it then?

The service that Jesus asks of us is not something idealistic, three feet above the ground; it's not a matter of having fine feelings about service, for if you look at the Gospel you will see that Jesus is speaking of a concrete kind of service, using your muscles, your legs, your head. To serve well you must, as we often say, "make yourself one" with the other. To live no longer turned in on yourself. To live the other, to seek to enter the other's heart, to know his feelings, share his joys, his anxieties, to carry his burdens. To make yourself one with him in everything except sin.

Are children wanting to play? Play with them. But, someone will object, what a waste of time it is, sitting there in front of the television watching this programme! What a waste of time spent going for walks. . . . No, it is not a waste of time! All is love. It is time you have gained, for we must make ourselves one with the other out of love. To make ourselves one out of love, not in order to convert others to Christ, not even for that, not even for any spiritual purpose. To make ourselves one with the other, full stop. That's what it's all about.

But that disinterested attitude conquers sooner or later. And what happens to the one who has been conquered? He also wants to love; he also wants to make himself one with others. And two are enough to give birth to Jesus in their midst. And then it is he himself who will give them the light and the strength to make the kingdom of God grow around them. It's the Bible which says: "Woe to those who are alone! And two united brothers are like a fortified tower!"

Certain attitudes, certain ways of doing things, certain ideas may require us to take a stand; we may need a certain Christian violence if we are to deserve the presence of Jesus.

I would say that it is better to direct violence against ourselves, against our ego. And indeed to create the conditions which will then merit the presence of Jesus in the midst, only that type of violence must be exercised. In the early days my companions and I found a trick which may still be useful today. We had made a sort of pact, to look at each other every morning as if it were for the first time, forgetting the other's faults. It was, so to speak, a 'pact of mercy'. That was violence if you like, since we were putting to death in our own minds the idea that we had of the others in order to see in everyone only Jesus.

Conducting oneself in this way brings some people the fullness of life, but you can feel as if you have been cut or wounded, sometimes violently, by those who refuse this way of behaving.

You speak quite rightly of being cut, for the Gospel, speaks of a cutting sword. However we must watch that the blade is not sharpened by our inept way of living the Gospel. When we have succeeded in establishing with a person a relationship which goes deep enough for us to be able to talk about the presence of God in our midst, we feel a joy so great that it is difficult to avoid a certain attachment to that joy. There is the danger. The attachment enslaves us and prevents us from loving others as we should. When we approach a new person our unity must be capable of losing itself, opening up to receive him or her. Otherwise that person finds egoism (however well-intentioned), and withdraws and strikes us. So that is a sword, but not the sword of the Gospel.

If on the other hand you are always full of love for everyone and the others do not return that love or even respond with hatred, that is the cutting blade of which the Gospel speaks.

You have written somewhere: "Do you know what we must do when we have loved beyond all measure? We must go on loving." But there are times when you know such suffering that your strength fails. Is not love a luxury for happy and secure people? The answer is often given that we must love suffering, love the cross. But how do we love it without falling into a kind of masochism, a greater evil?

There is only one way to follow Jesus. He himself revealed it to us: "If anyone would be my disciple let him renounce himself, take up his cross and follow me."

Renouncing oneself is painful, as is taking up the cross but it is the necessary way of following Jesus and the members of the Movement want to pursue it. Someone may say: "This is not human!" No! It is super-human, super-natural.

And so, when the members of the Movement are full of joy there is no problem, they enjoy it. But when they are suffering they transmute the suffering by a divine alchemy into love and that love makes them happy. So they are always seen to be joyous.

But then what does "loving the cross" or "suffering" mean?

Suffering is an element which our nature certainly cannot love. So it is not a matter of loving it with the emotions. We succeed in loving it with the will, but it is not a question of loving suffering for its own sake. Rather we love it because in welcoming it we see a possibility of following Jesus who said: "If you would follow me take up your cross daily." We can force ourselves to love suffering with our will with a view to following Jesus and helping him—as St. Paul says—to complete in us what is lacking in his Passion. If, like the saints we come to feel in some way an attraction to sorrow, it is not really a love of sorrow but a love of the man of sorrows, Jesus.

At the heart of the Movement is a very rich experience which proves that any human suffering finds itself again in the particular suffering of Jesus Forsaken. The solitary, the barren, the deceived, the failed, the weak, are they not like him? Are they not in his image, all those painful divisions between brothers, between the Churches, between political blocs in the grip of conflicting ideologies? And our materialistic secularised world the victim of every deviation, is it not a figure of Jesus who so to speak loses the awareness of God, who was made sin for us? In loving Jesus Forsaken, the Christian finds the reason and the strength not to flee from evils but to accept them, assume them and bring them their proper remedy. Jesus Forsaken is the key of unity, the secret of all renewal.

The spirituality of unity illuminates the Gospel in a special way but one of its pillars is day to day familiarity with the whole Gospel.

The alphabet only contains twenty-six letters but if you don't know them and if you don't learn a certain minimum of grammatical rules, you will remain illiterate your whole life. The Gospel is a little book but those who do not live the words that it contains remain illiterate Christians. The word of God is unique, incisive, majestic, eternal, universal; it is a place of the presence of God. To commune with it liberates, purifies, converts, brings consolation and joy, gives wisdom, produces works, calls people to follow Christ, but also attracts the hatred of the world. The word begets Christ in our souls.

So it is practically a food, comparable to the Eucharist and likewise distributed day to day.

Very frequently the members of the Movement feel spontaneously the necessity of receiving communion every day. That's one of the main causes of the very real unity which has formed within the Movement itself. Jesus in the Eucharist is the unifying link. It is through the Eucharist that men are in communion with God and among themselves. Before asking the

Father that "all may be one as you Father are in me, and I in you," Jesus had instituted the sacrament which made unity possible.

The name under which the Movement was officially approved in 1961 by John XXIII was "Opera di Maria" (The Work of Mary). Mary is not much loved today; she gets forgotten, or else people seem ashamed of her.

She is the mother. God has given her to us as a mother and we have always felt her to be our mother. Like a baby instinctively articulates its first word "Mama", so the Movement at its birth was incapable of giving itself a name other than that of Mary: "Work of Mary". It called its meetings "Mariapolis", its centres for spiritual training "Mariapolis Centres", its formation centres "Permanent Mariapolises."

Mary is the model for every member of the Movement, because as she had the primary function of being the physical mother of Christ, the Movement has that of spiritually bringing Christ into the world among men.

The Movement came into being among lay people but it attaches importance to the Magisterium and the Church's authority. It is encouraged by leaders in the various denominations where it exists and above all by the Pope and the Catholic Bishops; did not Pope John Paul II say to a large gathering of families: "My wish for the Church is that it may be you." What exactly does the ecclesiastical hierarchy represent for a Movement so lay in orientation?

Not only faith makes us believe in the presence of Jesus in his ministers, the Holy Father and the Bishops, but the experience of several decades has enabled us to verify the fact. It was St. Thérèse of Lisieux who said that God, in the night of this life, uses men "to hide his adorable presence, but he does not hide himself so well that we cannot guess he is there." And we have discovered this on all sorts of occasions. Behind those who represented the Church for us in the course of the various phases of the Movement's life, we have seen, almost with our physical eyes, Jesus leading us all the way: Jesus studying us, encouraging us, correcting us, guiding us. That has been a powerful experience. To all those who believe and live according to the word of God: "He who hears you, hears me," it is not difficult to have the profound conviction that Christ is present in the representatives of God beyond all their human weaknesses. The Gospel insists on this presence. The Fathers of the Church sing its praises and the saints no less. The Movement, because of this unshakeable faith has always remained grafted into the Pope and the Bishops like the branch in the vine, attentive not only to the orders but to the desires of the superiors. It is also to that that we attribute the world-wide explosion of the Movement, to that divine sap which has always been able to flow from the vine to the branches.

V
THE RAINBOW

We have spent long enough on the various salient features of the Focolare spirituality—although many fine things could still be said, of which some, fortunately, can be found in your works which have already been published. I should like now to take up another subject. Unity is a particular illumination of the Gospel, but what becomes of the light of the Gospel when it passes through the prism of unity?

We had the intuition one day that the love in our hearts was impelling us to the most diverse actions but which were all love and suddenly we found we were making a comparison with the light which passes through a prism or a drop of water and is refracted in the seven colours of the rainbow. Thus our love (if we do not want to fall into sentimentalism, enthusiasm or activism) must express itself in the most varied aspects of our existence, so that it can inspire all kinds of actions. The manifestations of the love of God are innumerable, as many as the actions of our lives, but we like to divide them into seven large categories.

Following the colours of the rainbow. I remember a certain congress of young people where you explained the demands of the

Christian life using that comparison which is not only a poetic image but also biblical.

I told them that God had put order in our lives after the manner of a rainbow. We need a degree of organisation but it must arise from love because the good thing about love is that it leaves us our freedom even when it is imposing order.

The rainbow has often been used as a symbol of peace and also of Mary. God has established on earth, amid the storms of this world, a spiritual rainbow which indicates to us what we have to do and which gives us norms to live by. The colours of the rainbow are different but they are all light. The same is true of every human action. People are terribly fond of dividing and subdividing their lives. We discover an aspect of life and become very keen on it and make it our ideal; football, cinema, painting, space travel, philosophical problems, social problems. We are so specialised in our predilections that we can't understand other people any more. It is only when God enters our lives and illuminates them through and through, like a sun placed in the centre, that the details harmonise with each other and we become true human beings: that is, each one a microcosm of the whole human race.

Let us begin then, if you will, with the first colour of the rainbow, with the red.

Love impels us to have everything in common. It sets in motion the sharing of material and spiritual resources. If we love our brothers and one of them is hungry without hesitation we give him the food which we have... The first Christians had everything in common. It was not compulsory, but having one's possessions in common was something to which they attached great importance.

Nowadays, I fear, Christians are more inclined to emphasise the optional nature of the thing than they are to imitate the first disciples of Jesus.

We must not confine ourselves to what is strictly obligatory but consider what pleases God, what he desires and, impelled by love, put our goods in common for the good of all. We must consider our possessions a patrimony from God which we have to administer for the benefit of everyone.

So that is red, which stands for love. In order to be a member of the Movement is it necessary to take the command of Jesus literally and go and sell everything you possess and give it to the poor?

It is not an obligation for anyone but the ideal would be for everything to circulate among us. This is what the young people of the Movement decided in their programme, which says: "What we are and what we have, spiritual resources and material possessions, we want *all* to be held in common among us, as a visible expression of the communion of saints and as a practical realisation of the verse of Scripture: "The whole group of believers was united in heart and soul; no one claimed for his own use anything that he had, as everything they had was held in common."

What they are setting themselves to live is true total Christian communion, a communion of life with possessions held entirely in common, which will not be slow in winning many others. It is a way of life which, if one day it is shared by a good part of Christendom and of the human race—since the world and especially the young are in a certain way prepared for this—might draw the whole Church and all humanity to become a community.

The holding of possessions in common among the first Christians had a splendid function; it demonstrated that they were all equal, that they were all brothers. Having things in common made for equality and we should thank God that he has made us rediscover equality.

Orange stands for witness, for the apostolate, so to speak. But it is an original apostolate in so far as it is founded on disinterested love. You often like to say that Mary did not go to see Elizabeth in order to sing her the "Magnificat" but to help her.

I must tell you again about the Bangwa. They were an animist tribe who seemed doomed to gradual extinction.

Among them was a tiny group of Christians, converted by the few missionaries who had ventured that far, who began to pray ardently for the Lord to help them. A year, two years passed, without an answer to their prayers.

After three years the Christians sent to the Bishop a sum of money which they had scraped together, to ask for the prayers of another tribe, more worthy than they, to obtain the desired grace. While all this was going on a doctor belonging to the Movement entered that region of the forest and was touched by the infant mortality which was reaching alarming proportions. The doctor installed himself in a hut like those of the others and began to care for the sick whenever they turned up. He asked for back-up and other young people in the Movement joined him. People came running to be treated and to save their children. Sometimes over a hundred patients would be treated in the course of a day.

Seeing what was happening the people realised that God had answered their prayers.

In 1968 when I visisted that territory which had once been jungle, infested with disease and wretchedness and savage beasts, I found a little city taking shape. We called it the "African Mariapolis". It consisted of a fine hospital, a college, a power station, and the numerous concrete houses of a population which had come to live in this little centre, and was expanding rapidly. Christians and animists rubbed shoulders at the opening of the hospital, they sang hymns of thanksgiving to the Lord and held a great feast with a solemn Mass and splendid colourful dances.

But the most astonishing and beautiful thing of all was that the doctors and their friends who had come to the aid of these people had done nothing other than work away in silence and yet the witness of their unity had brought about the beginning of a general conversion to God.

And today, after the baptism of Fon, whom you knew, at the time of his death, the chiefs of the tribe elected a young Christian to succeed him.

That's what unity produces. Jesus said: "That they may be one, so that the world may believe." The world of the Bangwa saw unity and believed. He who lives unity possesses the most powerful weapon for the conquest of the world.

The faithfulness of our witness had its roots in our unity. That's something we often assert. But now, now above all when there is so much to do, so much work, are we faithful to it? One thing is certain; if we remain united, come what may, in the name of Christ his spirit will penetrate and arouse the masses.

Let's speak about the yellow now.

We are still talking about love. But do you know what true love is, what its roots are?

True love—as you yourself put it—is rooted in God like a tree with the roots growing into Heaven and bearing fruit on earth.

The love which the yellow stands for is prayer, the scandal of prayer. Some people will laugh at us, but we will not let ourselves be paralysed by human respect. We would rather have "divine respect", respect for the things of God. The day when the Pharisees asked Jesus when the kingdom of God would come he replied: "The kingdom of God is within you." It is love, always love which impels us to unite ourselves more and more closely to Jesus, to tell him how we love him and to prove it to him by offering him our sufferings. Love induces us to ascend towards God, to achieve an increasingly perfect union with God.

If you are a very busy person and all your time is taken up with the daily grind, you have little time for prayer. How can you still maintain the link with God?

I would like to begin with a thought which may be a comforting one: I have never read in the Gospel that Jesus asked anyone to pray *for a long time*, on the contrary, he said: "When you pray, use few words." And immediately afterwards he taught the Our Father. And yet elsewhere in the scriptures we read that we should "pray *without ceasing*."

Now there's a contradiction! How can we pray without ceasing and yet not say long prayers?

If at every moment we are doing the will of God and not our own will, who is living in us? It is Christ, it is God who is living in us.

And Jesus himself in us can say to the Father: "Lord, I am your praise, because You and I are one; I share your own life." In this way our entire day will become an uninterrupted prayer.

Let's go on, if you will, to the green. Just as we must have a right idea of money and manage it for the common good, must we also have a right idea of our bodies and manage them for the common good.

Love impels us to remain in unity with others. It makes us live with a greater perfection, life in the "mystical body" as the Church teaches. Everyone is a complete entity, consisting of a soul and a body. And the body is also very important for a Christian. Just as in the past our forebears strove to build splendid Cathedrals for Jesus in the Eucharist, we must, since God lives in us take care of our bodies as of a temple in which he lives.

We must keep healthy in order to best serve our Creator. That is why we love sport. We don't consider it as an end in itself but as a way to have a sound mind which can gather all our faculties and carry out the plan for our life. A classical proverb speaks rightly of a "healthy mind in a healthy body."

And yet circumstances can sometimes go against our health. How do we react to illness or the prospect of death?

There again we must change our will, our mentality. In general when someone is ill, he complains and makes the whole family anxious. But we must accept suffering with serenity because God has sent it and, if our pain permits, we should smile. Smiling at illness is the best means of giving sense and value to an experience which comes sooner or later in the existence of everyone.

The same disposition will also enable us to face up to death, which everyone fears so much and is usually synonymous with mourning and tears.

At the hour of death we must leave the body to wait for the resurrection but the soul does not cease to live for its God, who will never fail it. Saint Francis talked of "Sister death." We say to it: "Come friend, open door to Paradise, you are welcome, and we shall see at last those whom we love who have crossed the river, with all our brothers and sisters who have gone to heaven, and all the saints."

Death will not make us afraid, because Jesus has shared our mortal flesh.

Proper management of one's physical strength, one's health, without being over-attached to it and without neglecting it, is not really possible except in relationship with others. Individual health cannot be separated from the health, if we can put it like this, of the "social body".

Individual physical health is not enough. We also want the health of the mystical body of Christ which is made up of all Christians joined to one another and to Christ by love. The vitality of the Mystical Body keeps all the members in unity and makes us have a single body and a single soul, like the first Christians.

When something gets out of order in the organs of a body it loses its health. Likewise when concord is lacking among Christians the mystical body is ill. Jesus has left us a remedy for disunity, the Eucharist.

This gift of Jesus is so precious that we must receive communion as often as possible.

We are going through the rainbow, every band of which is a colour of love. Having possessions in common, the apostolate, the spiritual life, health, and now: what does the blue stand for?

It is an aspect of love which leads us to gather together, to assemble as Church. Before they had churches built of stone the first Christians formed a living Church. It must be the same with us.

But in concrete terms we also need a stone building to protect that living Church.

Of course we need a house. It need not necessarily be rich—Jesus was born in a stable. But what house is lit by a light more resplendent than the Star of Bethlehem? And what house was as beautiful as that which sheltered the immaculate heart of his mother who adored him and the respectful, faithful Joseph who had the task of guarding the first dwelling of Jesus? That is the beauty with which we would want to embellish our house. We know that Jesus must live there. Yes Jesus present among us who are gathered in his name.

Jesus, who is love and beauty incarnate, must be surrounded by love and harmony. Our house must be kept like Mary kept the house at Nazareth, the dwelling place of the Incarnate Word; it must be kept with such cleanliness and order and good taste that a chance visitor finding it empty would exclaim with surprise: "Whoever lives here is not of this world." Yes, because Jesus has his own inimitable style and he has consecrated the walls and the objects which have welcomed him and these walls and these objects seem to speak of his presence.

When we return home and find the mark of Jesus who has been living among us, we are at once recalled by that divine harmony to full and complete unity. And Jesus can continue to live among us, to inspire us in our new life, to suggest plans to us to encourage us to continue or to begin again if we have ceased loving.

You attach great importance to the style of dress of the members of Christ, which we are, and you do not exclude a reference to fashion.

If Christ lives in us and among us, our clothing must reflect the simplicity and harmony of God.

The elegance and fashionableness that we want are not to be confused with extravagance or luxury, but seek to achieve the perfection of an original line corresponding to the innate personality of each one. "Consider the lilies of the field and the birds of the air; even Solomon in all his glory was not arrayed like one of these." If we are living out the Gospel, fashion will be our way of rejoining the beauty of nature.

You used an expression which, as you know touches me personally very much: "Jesus is beauty incarnate."

God has always been shown to us as good, just, almighty, rarely as beautiful. Our vocation is to show the beauty of God. It is not in vain that we are awaiting paradise where everything will appear clothed in beauty. Christ must be the model of the Christian's life in all its expressions, including those which may seem in a certain sense to be marginal to religion.

As is the case with the work of the artist.

The place of art is the soul of the artist. There he contemplates an impression, an idea, which he will later express in outward form. Within the limits of his infinite smallness as a man vis-a-vis his creator, and thus the infinite diversity of the two creations, taking all the difference of scale into account the artist is a "re-creator." He creates anew, revealing through his works the infinite beauties of the creation—of which one of the loveliest features is the soul of a great artist.

The masterpiece of God is the human soul, and the artist when he expresses the best of himself introduces others through his art to the contemplation of God's masterpiece.

People rediscover themselves in their own deepest nature, which is Christ present in them; Christ, who is not only truth and life, but also beauty.

Let us leave that colour and consider the Christian life in another light, the indigo of our rainbow. Recently a university has sprung up within the Movement. How do you explain that, since the Movement appears to many to grant only secondary importance to study and to distrust intellectualism?

To understand what God expects of us in the area of study we must, as always, go back to our history. The first significant fact is this: in 1944, at the dawn of the Movement, as I have already told you, driven by an inner impulse I left my studies and consigned my philosophy books "to the attic." Now while the external cause of that decision was the initial development of the Movement, and my obligation to be there all the time, it had, none the less, a much deeper motive. I was thirsting after truth and had just realised that it was absurd to seek it in philosophy alone when I could find it in Jesus, the Truth incarnate. So I left my studies to follow him, the Christ, and possess in following him all the fulness of life. In that, I was to find a new light since God manifests himself to those who love him and follow him.

That episode must be seen as the first fruits of what was to become in time a rich harvest in the Movement. We were going to see a light shine forth indeed but it was to be the soul of a life. We were going to speak of schools but the day would come when the Movement—which we have already been able to consider under different aspects, such as Work of Mary, Family of Mary, City of Mary etc.—could also be regarded as the School of Mary.

Had you been thinking since the early years of a school like that which has begun, the one we call the U.P.M.?*

The Movement was born among a small number of people, and from the very first days this little group was called a school, more precisely "the school of fire." It was, in fact a school; it functioned like a school, but it was an original kind of school. It had neither books, nor classrooms, nor studies. No, that group was a school because there was a Teacher there. Jesus was there, living among the pupils.

So great, so divine was this reality that it made that school unique, beyond all comparison with any other. Not only that but if Jesus was the teacher, his lessons were so special that they were of quite another order than those of the world's greatest teachers. I even used to say that sometimes it seemed that Jesus was teaching us things which could pass for folly in the eyes of others, even the wisest, such as when, for example, he showed us the value of suffering. Or it could seem that his teaching was not even a doctrine if by doctrine you understand a purely intellectual reality.

One thing is certain however. He who lived among us was God and so he was capable of answering all the questions that men of all times might ask him.

So the light came, an abundance of it. It illuminated the spirituality which God expected of you and it fashioned day by day the development of the Movement.

*U.P.M. stands for *Università Popolare Mariana* which provides theology courses for members of the Movement.

We called that light wisdom. And Christian wisdom has not been lacking since it has raised up and ordered this Movement in which the Church has recognised a Work of God. Now we realised that it was fundamentally upon wisdom that our new studies stood. When God is calling us to extend his kingdom what use would a knowledge be which is not illuminated by wisdom?

And how do we obtain wisdom?

In order to obtain wisdom we must live with Jesus present in our midst. He is wisdom. So let us be at unity among ourselves, widen our heart so that it is open to the whole of the Movement; let us be in perfect unity with the Church and with its representatives both outside and within the Movement. Then Jesus will be with us and with him will be wisdom.

In the rule of the Movement, in the chapter entitled "Study" can be read: "The focolarini will strive to gain true Christian wisdom. . . ." And further on ". . .wisdom accompanied not only by appropriate religious knowledge but also by all secular learning useful to that end." So there is wisdom and study but we grant the latter a precise function, that of accompanying wisdom.

However, since learning can also inflate and extinguish the spirit, our rule adds that ". . .the focolarini shall apply themselves to studies but in such a way that these are not an obstacle to the spirit of God. . . ." And yet since well organised, well directed studies can on the other hand serve the kingdom of

God, the rule lays down that the focolarini shall make their studies become a way of loving God and their neighbour. While I had abandoned my studies since 1943-44, some years later I felt the desire to take up my books again and study theology. I felt the need to put down solid foundations for the numerous intuitions that had come to me during that period. That same year Pasquale Foresi expressed his intention of becoming a priest and in him I saw someone who was going to be able to engage in a course of study. It is also since that time that the focolarini and other members of the Movement have started to enter the various theology faculties.

You have realised from the beginning that studies should include both secular and religious disciplines.

Secular studies are necessary of course. But we want to immerse ourselves in them because we take as our model Jesus, who was not only a priest but the complete man, a carpenter for thirty years and competent in his profession.

So we must acquire the technical knowledge useful to our profession and work at perfecting that all our lives.

Where the religious aspect is concerned—since the Movement finds its charter in the testament of Jesus, "That all may be one,"—the end of our studies will be to deepen our understanding of the truths relating to the mystical body of Christ, the whole Christ.

With Christian wisdom accompanied by theology and the human sciences we hope to see the doctrine of the mystical body developing, a doctrine which finds an incomparable teacher in the Virgin Mary. She is indeed the mother of the members of the mystical body, the mother of the Church. Mary is the 'social person' par excellence; Jesus was born of her, the mystical body of Christ is born of her. That is why we already like to call the doctrine of the mystical body which the members of the Movement will formulate, the doctrine of Mary.

The U.P.M. will not however develop a doctrine of Mary.

The School of Mary will not consider mariology as a chapter of theology; rather all theology will be revised and Mary will be the starting point.

This doctrine will have to take into consideration all the results already obtained by the work to which the theologians have applied themselves hitherto in the Church in order to bring them its own contribution, the fruit of studies conducted with Jesus present among us.

In that school teachers and students will have to strive to live all the virtues and above all, humility in order to be able to listen to other spiritualities so that they can receive what each one has to teach them. In this way they will produce something which I call a Marian synthesis.

The participation of religious spiritually linked to the Movement will be of great help. We will have through them vital contact with the sons of St. Francis, St. Dominic, St. Ignatius etc. They express the thought of their spiritual Schools and in that way, realising the testament of Jesus among us, we will be serving on the doctrinal plane as well, the Mystical Body of Christ today.

We have come now to the last colour of the spectrum: violet.

The Movement is widespread in numerous nations in different continents but all its members are closely linked one to another. This is essential for us. We keep up a frequent correspondence so that we can all be perfectly one. To feel that we are many but "one body"—to use the powerful expression of St. Paul—and to live accordingly is also one of the demands of love. That is what the violet represents.

The circulation of news within the Movement is perhaps one of the aspects which the attentive observer finds most striking. I need only mention that every two weeks there is a conference call by telephone which brings into direct communication a good part of the inner group of members of the Movement in five continents. In this way they are informed of the latest matters of spiritual interest and the most important news. This conference call is immediately relayed by a newsletter to all those who could not be present for the call.

If the Movement has one characteristic I think it is precisely that feature of keeping our members informed. Of course all aspects of life are important.

In general militant Christians try to communicate their ideas to others; they know that they need a house, money to meet expenses etc. but we too often forget to share with all our joys and sorrows, to carry burdens, to spread the good news of success or that of the inevitable persecutions which the world holds in store for us.

Oh no, the world is small and communication is possible. Alaska, Australia, Peru, China, Africa, Japan, Italy, England . . . all the world of the focolarini is here in our heart. Not only because we are praying for them but because we feel ourselves strengthened by the magnificent example of all, we are comforted in times of failure, we never feel alone. If the human proverb is true which says, "unity is strength", what of our world-wide supernatural unity?

We have looked together at life under these different lights. Perhaps it is important to return to the comparison which has been guiding us and say that if the Christian life can split like white light into many different concrete expressions which are all consequences of love, it is only in living all these colours in a balanced way that we re-discover the white light, the authentic Christian life. To us, one aspect is as valuable as another, none has an advantage over the others, but all deserve the same care, the same faithfulness, the same investment from the heart of effort and intelligence.

In fact the idea of a total consecration to God in the service of all is illuminated by life in these seven aspects. Every moment of the day, every action completed, enters one or other of these aspects and must be the fruit of love.

VI
THE WORLD CAN CHANGE

In 1958 you made two journeys out of Italy (perhaps your first two long visits abroad) one to visit the World Fair in Brussels and the other to Lourdes on the occasion of the centenary of the apparitions. At a time when I was first coming into contact with the Movement this bringing together of these two things seemed highly symbolic to me; for even if your innermost preferences were no doubt with the humble grotto in Massabielle where a heavenly reality showed itself to a simple peasant girl, you none the less did not disdain the miracles of technology and the human knowledge which the nations of the world proudly displayed before the astonished eyes of so many of your contemporaries.

Right from the first step the Movement appeared to me to be about both spiritual renewal and social engagement.

It would seem that for you spirituality and incarnation have to go hand in hand. We cannot want to change ourselves without wanting to change the world.

The Focolare Movement can now be found in more than 150 nations and you have had the chance personally to visit a large number of countries. Are you optimistic about the future of humanity?

We need only take one look at the face of humanity in our times to draw the extremely bitter conclusion that it is marked by the shadow of corruption, the lines of fragmentation.

Every day the newspapers, the radio, the television supply tedious lists of these revealing signs. We know that political, ideological, military and economic divisions dominate our planet. Human rights are violated. Materialism is spreading in all its forms. Entire nations are under the yoke of other nations. Misery, hunger, illiteracy, still afflict the poor nations. Unemployment, drug abuse, violence and pornography are invading the rich countries. Corruption in political circles is becoming normal. Moral values are being undermined. More and more terrible weapons are being produced and wars are still breaking out. Terrorism still reigns. Organised crime is on the increase. The family has undergone heavy assaults. Women are no longer in their place anywhere. Lack of respect for the natural world is having serious consequences. Urbanisation is crowding millions of souls into inhuman, octopus-like cities. Materialistic cultures are triumphing. Permissive cultures are spreading. . . .

These are some alarming aspects of the breakdown to which humanity seems to be moving. And it is these aspects which are coming more and more into evidence.

But no doubt everything that is happening in the world is not totally negative?

Men, women, young people, government associations, the Catholic Church and the other Churches, the faithful of other religions and people of good will are reacting purposefully.

A vast campain to alert people to the threat to peace is developing at an international level. Initiatives to ensure respect for the rights of the human person are multiplying and the oppression of certain nations by other nations is being condemned. People want to join the fight against hunger, help the Third World, marginal groups, the aged, the handicapped. Among young people there is also a quest for spiritual values and a certain rejection of the consumer society. The excesses of the permissive society are provoking reactions against it. Groups are getting together to combat drug abuse and crime. The ecology movement is spreading. The great development of science and technology and in the field of communications is opening perspectives hitherto unimaginable, of instantaneous exchange of information among men everywhere and mutual understanding.

It's true, countless efforts are made in the world—in every domain and in all directions—to remedy the characteristic ills of our society so as to give it a new look. All initiatives in favour of the good of mankind and all manifestations of solidarity and fraternity, even if they are merely human, make a great contribution to that cause. They are laudable efforts which we must encourage, share and support. But are they enough?

Even if you attempt with the best will in the world to improve the human condition, you don't always succeed. The fact is that people, in spite of all their good intentions, do not have to wait long before they experience their own limits; most often internal forces and external circumstances lead them to indifference, opting out, isolation and selfishness.

Why?

Because often each person discovers that he must struggle alone and he can rely only upon his own strength.

And here is what would appear to be the specific contribution which our Movement can make in every environment in which it is present, in every country where it is at work; to say and to prove that we are never alone in the outsize task of renewing society, restoring it to hope and confidence and offering it lasting benefits in proportion to its needs.

Even in our concrete day to day life with its problems and its plans, with its sufferings and its joys we are not alone. A Father is there walking with us.

We do not always draw all the conclusions from that certainty and we lead our own life, we build the earthly city, we want to renew the world as if we had to do the whole difficult task by ourselves; whereas heaven is on our side and if we have a Father, he also knows how to give us—as Igino Giordani used to affirm—besides the bread of heaven, earthly bread, and all we need.

Differences, sometimes of a most glaring kind, exist on the social level. Rich and poor still confront each other on opposing sides.

One of the greatest certainties that our Movement has acquired during these forty years of its life, a certainty which derives from daily experience, is that in living the Good News we spark off the Gospel revolution in the world and that means that we also spark off the most powerful social revolution.

We believe with Mary—and thanks be to God we have seen this being realised in many parts of our planet—that the law of the Gospel lived can really "fill the hungry with good things" and "send the rich away empty." We are witnesses that the words of Jesus, "Blessed are the poor", and that other saying, severe and threatening, "Woe to the rich", if taken seriously, give a tremendous impetus to the re-establishment of social balance.

We are familiar also with the problems of unemployment, the aged, groups on the edge of society, the handicapped, famine, and the formidable challenge of the Third World.

The whole of Christian history teaches us that the page of the Gospel concerning the last judgement of every Christian brings some surprising results.

For Jesus will say to us at the last judgement: I was hungry in your husband, in your children, in the population of India, and you, seeing me in them gave them food.

I was thirsty, I was naked every morning in your children, as in your brothers and sisters of many nations where living conditions are inhuman, and you, always seeing me in them, clothed me with what you had. I was an orphan, hungry and sick in that child from down the street, and in the people of such and such a country laid waste by a typhoon, threatened by cholera, and you did everything you could to help me.

You put up with your mother-in-law or your nervous wife, your angry workers or your insensitive boss, because you were convinced that perfect social justice can arise only from love among people; and this you did because you saw me in everyone.

You visited me in that relative of yours who had been put in prison, you prayed for those who live under oppression and whose most intimate thoughts and feelings have been violated, and it was I to whom you were bringing help when you did the impossible for them.

Giving as the Gospel demands, ("give and you will receive") guarantees in return, "good measure, pressed down, shaken and overflowing." Our Movement has often found this to be true. Knowing how to give is the only concrete attitude which can relieve those who are in want, those who suffer hunger, loneliness, those who need everything.

In the world there is division, the arms race, wars and terrorism.

Who can deny that loving one's neighbour as the Gospel teaches, loving one's enemy, the new commandment, lived on a grand scale among mankind would be the best antidote to all these serious evils, these terrible dangers, and would constitute the best guarantee of peace?

And drugs, pornography, violence? Why does man degrade himself in this way?

Because he wants pleasure out of everything. Now we, who try to live our Christianity, know that the adventure of the Gospel of love, life lived for others, or better "living the other;" is the source of an immense and very pure happiness. Let us help as many people as possible to taste that fullness of joy which Jesus promised and those sad epidemics will disappear.

You also mentioned the crisis in family life.

The family is nothing other than a bond of love, a mystery of love; the love of husband and wife, motherly, fatherly love, the love of children for their parents and brothers and sisters, the love of grandchildren for their grandparents, aunts, cousins; the family is held together by love. If the family is in a state of crisis today it is because there is less love around. Where love dies the family decays.

The God of Love is familiar with the family; it is he who fashioned it as a masterpiece of love; it is he also who can heal it through love.

The family today needs a strong dose of love. Our Movement must stir up love among members of all the families it meets.

Is it possible to add anything further or to lay down guidelines for such a vast programme?

This is my feeling: to restore the family to its true image, to restore its splendour, besides speeches, exhortations and directives there is one radiant and universal example: the Family of Nazareth. That is the one that every family in the world, both now and in times to come can take as its ideal model. And not only the families: every member of the family can draw inspiration from the example of the Holy Family in order to know how to behave, what attitudes to take, how to relate to others, what qualities to cultivate.

And feminism?

Every woman can find in Mary the model of what she should be, equality with men, and her own identity. Every woman can see, realised in the wife of Joseph her deep desire to be a participant at the centre of things, and can learn how to gather the family circle around her in order to distribute for the good of all the riches which are proper to her; the capacity for sacrifice, the inner life which makes her sure of herself, the sense of the divine that distinguishes her, the innate need to radiate beauty, innocence, purity.

Our contemporaries are no longer conscious of belonging to the one political community, with its duties and privileges.

Our experience is that in putting into practice the word of Christ, "Give to Caesar the things that belong to Caesar. . ." we have the best guarantee that the laws of the state, those that are not contrary to the will of God, are observed.

You have painted a vivid picture of our world. You are aware that good will is not enough and yet you pick up so many signs of hope.

Our human life, often so monotonous and slow moving can change direction and take wings. The world can change. Despite the evident breakdown in many areas of life we are on our way perhaps to a new era.

Standing beside those who today are seeking the good of humanity, and deeply united with them in purpose, we think that our own contribution towards the renewal of the world is to offer an experience of the Gospel with all the repercusssions that it can have on our way of life individually and socially.

If, among people like us—belonging to all sorts of different nations and races, from every part of the globe, speaking lots of different languages—if among us love, harmony, peace and happiness are possible, and if we lack no necessity, why should it not be the same for many others?

I would like to underline again a certain truth, a Gospel truth, which the Holy Spirit has drawn particularly to our attention right from the beginning of the Movement, and which we are called to realise by total commitment to it. It is the truth that where people are united in Christ's name, he is present. He is not only present in the tabernacles of our churches, nor only in people who are called to proclaim his message or sustain his Church. No! He is also there among us all! He is in our midst, among his people.

It is the inspiring truth that Christ is a reality, that he did not just have one brief contact of a few years with the world two thousand years ago, but he is risen and present in our midst every time that we love each other as he desires us to do, sharing our hopes, aspirations, necessities, pains, struggles, victories; he is present: "I am with you always, to the end of time."

Of course that presence is very important. But why do you emphasise that particular aspect of the Gospel so much?

We, who are called to build the earthly city must, in a certain manner continue the work of the Creator. Now to whom did the Father turn when he created the world? It says in the Gospel: "In the beginning was the Word. . . . All things were made through him."

All things were made through him, through the Word. So the Word had a role in creation. The plan for humanity was in him as he created.

And we, who desire to contribute to the renewal of the world, to whom shall we turn in order that we may build the earthly city in harmony with the creation? Who can best show us the way?

We will turn to Jesus, the Incarnate Word. And if he is present in our midst that will be easier. Who better than he can suggest what we should do, support us in what we have already undertaken, correct us, or indeed give us the courage to start again from scratch.

But the presence of Jesus in our midst is equally important for another reason. We know that humanity bears within itself a wound that cannot be healed: a yearning for the spiritual. It is tormented by the divine, spurred on by the infinite, drawn by the eternal.

We know that even if people were to succeed in renewing all humanity, in building a new world, their hearts would not yet be filled with everything they desire.

We are made for a life that never dies. It must be emphasised, therefore, that people whilst building the earthly city, can henceforth build something that will not pass away, for they can contribute by their own work to the "new heaven and new earth" which await them.

Along with the cosmos, Christ has in effect also redeemed human achievement.

The universe will not be destroyed, but transfigured. There will be no rupture between this life and the beyond, but a continuity.

The excellent fruits of nature and equally those of our industry—that is all that we build day after day—will not only not disappear, but we will find them again later, purified from all stain, illumined and transfigured.

This is a glorious truth, a sublime and consoling vision of the vocation of humanity to transform the earth by its own work. But there is a condition. The works of humanity in the world will remain only if they are founded on the commandment of love.

But who will assure us that our efforts are being well spent in that way? Who will tell us if we are really building on the rock of love and therefore assure us that what we are making will not perish?

Again it will be Jesus in our midst. Jesus in our midst will guarantee it; he it is who transforms every society great or small, making it at the same time a cell of the earthly city and a cell of the heavenly city.

In effect, he is wholly present where there is love. It is a gift of God and, at the same time, the fruit of the mutual love that we must put at the basis of all our activities.

Jesus in our midst! In him then can be found the plan of a new humanity. In him is the guarantee that what we do will endure.

How could we fail to be attracted by the road we are on and the way that lies ahead? And could we do other than think and dream of a new humanity when we have with us the one of whom the Spirit could say: "Behold, I am making all things new?"

With our Movement, with the spirit which impels it, God has given us a powerful means of leading mankind to hope that we can set out for what will no doubt come—if God wills and we want it—the civilisation of the year 2000, that is, the "civilisation of love."

I would like, as would you I am sure, to be already there in the year 2000 to see that civilisation of love.

EPILOGUE

Since the 7th December 1943, forty years ago now, your life has been very full, rich in events both happy and sad. We have recalled some of them, perhaps the most significant, perhaps not the most important; they can't always be expressed in words. You said at the beginning of these conversations that on the day of your solitary consecration, you had not the faintest idea of the consequences of your action. Have you no regrets? If it was possible, would you put the clock back?

No! Although I am very conscious that I could have done everything better. No. What has happened in these forty years is too great. A little twig, already flowering has been grafted into the tree which is the Church and has itself become Church. The graft took, and the instruments which God used are of no importance. What counts is the Church, and we, poor and small as we are, have the joy of enriching it with a new light, gracing it with new blossom. And all this has happened thanks to those who answered to the gift of God, thanks to the charism, that talent which we had to multiply, thanks also to our weaknesses, our naivety, our inadequacies. Not because our weaknesses, naiveties and inadequacies are good things in themselves, but because, having always believed that everything that happens is for good to those who love God, we found that weakness, ingenuousness and shortcomings became useful material for God to work with; indeed they became our greatest strength—glorifying in our weaknesses as St. Paul said. And they enabled people to see that our work is indeed a work of God.

But that graft could have failed to take. We were free. So it seems sensible to me not to want to go backwards but rather to thank God for these years; we can never do so enough.

I have thought many times that when I died I would take with me into the next life a certain joy, the joy of having contributed to a work of God which will still be there after I have gone, because it is Church. Even so, we still need God to assure us of his protection because we could still spoil everything.

And what of the future of the Movement?

How could we foresee it? We will have to tread in Jesus' footsteps. The builder's plan is in Heaven not on earth. Up till now we have followed the architect moment by moment, day by day.

And now, forward! Who knows what is awaiting us? Certainly it will all be nothing other than love. Even in my most optimistic forecasts I could never have imagined on December 7th 1943 what I am seeing today.

Praise be to God, glory to Mary, Queen of a kingdom which has—quite literally—invaded the world.

CHIARA

May 1944. A massive air-raid on Trent. Chiara Lubich and some of her young companions are sheltering in a dark cellar lit by a candle. She opens the Gospel at Jesus's prayer before his death: 'Father . . . may they all be one'. They understand that it is for this very page of the Gospel that they have been born. Jesus's request for the deepest unity among his followers became the ideal of their lives and of the Focolare Movement. 'May they all be one so that the world will believe' is its method.

Edwin Robertson is a Baptist Pastor in London. An author of international recognition he has been Director of the World Association of Christian Broadcasting of the BBC. A former Study Secretary of the United Bible Societies he is perhaps better known for his translations and editing of the English works of the distinguished German Pastor Dietrich Bonhoeffer.